The Book of Korean Poetry

THE BOOK *of*
Korean Poetry

Songs of Shilla & Koryŏ

TRANSLATED & ANNOTATED

by KEVIN O'ROURKE

UNIVERSITY

OF IOWA

PRESS

IOWA CITY

University of Iowa Press,
Iowa City 52242
Copyright © 2006 by the
University of Iowa Press
http://www.uiowa.edu/uiowapress
All rights reserved
Printed in the United States of America
Published under the support of the Korea
Literature Translation Institute
Design by Richard Hendel

The University of Iowa Press is a member of
Green Press Initiative and is committed to
preserving natural resources.

Printed on acid-free paper

Cataloging-in-Publication
data on file at the Library of Congress.

06 07 08 09 10 P 5 4 3 2 1

CONTENTS

ACKNOWLEDGMENTS

I would like to acknowledge the support of the Korean Culture and Arts Foundation and the Korean Literature Translation Institute in making the translations.

Poems in this collection have previously appeared in *The Shijo Tradition* (Jung Eum Sa, 1987), *Tilting the Jar, Spilling the Moon* (Universal Publishing Company, 1989; Dedalus, 1993), *Singing Like a Cricket, Hooting Like an Owl* (Cornell East Asia Program, 1995), *Mirrored Minds: A Thousand Years of Korean Poetry* (Eastward Publications, 2001), *The Book of Korean Shijo* (Harvard University Asia Center, 2002), *A Hundred Love Poems from Old Korea* (Global Oriental, 2005), *Korea Herald, Korea Times, Korea Journal,* and *Koreana.*

This book is the first part of a project that has been ongoing for thirty years. I dedicate it to my three brothers, Frank, Chas, and Joe; to their wives, Rose, Marie, and Anne; and to their children. I dedicate it also to the Columbans who gave me the latitude to spend my life in literature and to those who worked with me on the project, especially Pak Kidawk, Han Kyongshim, and Katherine Lee. Finally, I dedicate it to the many friends whose support through the years made the volume possible.

If you wonder why Korea is in the blood,
look to the heart, to friends that endure,
to loyalty green as pine and bamboo,
to flowers that have bloomed in the snow.

A NOTE ON TEXTS AND SOURCES

With the exception of the *hanshi* selections, the texts for this volume for the most part chose themselves. Only a few pre-Shilla poems are extant. The fourteen Shilla *hyangga* are included. The major Koryŏ *kayo* are also included; only a few short, incantatory pieces that defied translation have not been attempted. Less than twenty Koryŏ *shijo* have claims to authenticity, and fourteen of them are included here. The selection *of hanshi* texts, however, posed a major problem. While the vast number of extant *hanshi* forced me to rely on the judgment of the Korean commentators in terms of what poets and poems to include, I tried to select only poems that I felt had intrinsic merit and universal appeal. The book has a large selection of Yi Kyubo poems for several reasons. First, he is the best *hanshi* poet of the Koryŏ dynasty and arguably the best *hanshi* poet in Korean history; second, he has left several thousand poems; and third, the planned companion volume on the poetry of the Chosŏn dynasty gives equivalent coverage to major poets such as Chŏng Ch'ŏl, Yun Sŏndo, and Kim Sujang.

The texts for the pre-Shilla songs are taken from *Uri kojŏn shiga hanmadang* (1994), compiled by Kim Yong and published by Hyemun sŏ'gwan.

The *hyangga* texts are taken from two sources: Kang Kil'un's *Hyangga shin haedok yŏn'gu* (1995), published by Hangmun sa; and Kim Wanjin's *Hyangga haedokpŏp yŏn'gu* (1980), published by Seoul University Press.

The Koryŏ *kayo* texts are from Pak Pyŏngch'ae's *Koryŏ kayoŭi ŏsŏk yŏn'gu* (1994), published by Kukhak charyo wŏn.

The *hanshi* texts are from a number of sources: *Taedong shisŏn*, published by Hangmin ch'ulp'ansa (1992); *Uriŭi myŏngshi* (1990), compiled by Kim Chonggil and Lee Ŏryŏng and published by Tonga ch'ulp'ansa; and *Uri yetshi* (1986), compiled by Hŏ Kyŏngjin and published by Ch'ŏnga ch'ulp'ansa. Extensive use was also made of Hŏ Kyŏngjin's *Han'gukŭi hanshi* series, published by P'yŏngmin sa, specifically the volumes on Ch'oe Ch'iwŏn, Yi Chehyŏn, and poems by Koryŏ monks. Yi Kyubo's poems are taken from *Tongguk Yi Sangguk chip* (Collected Works of Minister Yi from the Eastern Kingdom).

Han'guk shijo taesajŏn (1992), edited by Pak Ŭlsu and published by Asea munhwasa, is the most complete guide to *shijo* literature currently available.

This two-volume book has texts, notes, classical allusions, and sources for 4,736 poems. The texts are arranged alphabetically. *Shijo munhak sajŏn* (1974), edited by Chŏng Pyŏng'uk and published by Shin'gu munhwasa, is still a very convenient collection of *shijo* for the non-Korean reader. It contains 2,376 poems arranged alphabetically as well as sources, notes on difficult words and phrases, classical allusions, and information on poets. The major shortcoming of *Shijo munhak sajŏn* is that it is out of date in terms of texts and information on poets. In the last twenty years the canon of *shijo* has almost doubled. Shim Chaewan's *Yŏkdae shijo chŏnsŏ* has 3,335 poems (with all the variant readings), and his *Shijoŭi munhŏnjŏk yŏn'gu* is an exhaustive account of sources. Shim's books do not have allusions to classical sources, however; nor do they have explanations of difficult words and phrases, though versions of the poems in modern *han'gŭl* script are provided.

The numbers indicating original *shijo* texts refer to *Shijo munhak sajŏn* because it is the most convenient of the comprehensive anthologies and also because I used it to do the translations. Texts differ from anthology to anthology, so it seemed safer to cite the text that I used. It is a simple matter to proceed from any *chang* in the original Korean to the corresponding poem in the other anthologies.

Romanization of *han'gŭl* follows the McCune-Reischauer system. *Si*, however, is transcribed as *shi* (*shijo* and Shilla, for example, as opposed to *sijo* and Silla). The hyphen in Korean given names is dropped. An apostrophe indicates syllable breaks in cases of possible confusion in pronunciation (Kwang'uk, for example, instead of Kwanguk).

Pinyin is used to transcribe Chinese terms.

Early Songs

Korea's history is divided into four periods: the Three King-doms—Koguryŏ (37 BC–AD 668), Shilla (57 BC–AD 668), and Paekche (18 BC–AD 660); Unified Shilla (668–935); Koryŏ (935–1392); and Chosŏn (1392–1910). Koguryŏ was the largest of the Three Kingdoms. Its territory extended from south of the Han River into Manchuria. The men were known as brave warriors and accomplished horsemen. Paekche was the most prosperous of the three, boasting trade links with China and Japan. Koguryŏ and Shilla quarreled constantly. Eventually Shilla employed a Chinese army to conquer Koguryŏ and Paekche and unified the country for the first time. These were the main kingdoms in Korea's early history, but the peninsula was not divided among them. Minor kingdoms existed side by side. Unified Shilla was an era of great cultural accomplishment, during which an attempt was made to establish an ideal Buddhist state. The last two hundred years of the dynasty, however, were marked by weakness and decadence. In 900 Kyŏn Hwŏn, a rebel leader, established Latter Paekche; and in 901 Kung'ye, another rebel leader, set up Latter Koguryŏ. Wang Kŏn, first minister of Kung'ye, overthrew his lord and succeeded in overwhelming Shilla with the support of landlords and merchants. King Kyŏngsun of Shilla abdicated in 935. The following year Wang Kŏn conquered Latter Paekche and unified the Korean peninsula for the second time.

Thus began the Koryŏ dynasty, from which modern Korea takes its name. While Wang Kŏn was a distinguished leader, his successors were not of the same caliber. With the passage of time, Koryŏ became weak and corrupt, undermined by conflict between civilian and military factions in the government. The kingdom suffered a series of invasions by the northern barbarian tribes and continuous acts of piracy by the Japanese. The Koryŏ kings eventually became no more than figureheads. In 1392 General Yi Sŏnggye set up the Chosŏn dynasty. Chosŏn brought the full flowering of Confucian culture, which had radical consequences for the administration of the country and also for the nature of poetry discourse.

According to *Samguk yusa* (Memorabilia of the Three Kingdoms, an important source work on history, folklore, literature, and religion compiled in

1285 by the monk Iryŏn), the earliest Korean poetry was religious, magical, and incantatory. It was ordered around rituals to propitiate spirits and to appeal for good harvests, accompanied by singing and dancing. These festive celebrations continued late into the night. Kim Hŭnggyu quotes from the "History of Wei" section of *The History of the Three Kingdoms* (*Samguk chi*; Chinese: *Sanguo zhi*) by Chen Shou (223–297)[1]:

> On New Year's Day . . . the people . . . of Puyŏ hold a festival in honour of the heavens. At this festival . . . they drink, dance and sing endlessly.
>
> In the kingdom of Mahan, the people hold a festival in honor of the gods after finishing the spring planting in May. They drink and dance for days on end at this festival.
>
> The people of Koguryŏ like to sing and dance. Men and women in villages throughout the country gather every night to sing and dance.
>
> In Chinhan, people like to dance and sing while drinking and playing the *kŏmun'go*.

Korean people loved to dance and sing. Unfortunately, very few early texts have survived: a few pre-Shilla poems (composed in or translated into Chinese characters), fourteen Shilla *hyangga* recorded in *Samguk yusa*, and eleven Koryŏ *hyangga* recorded in *Kyunyŏ chŏn* (Life of Kyunyŏ, the biography of an eminent Buddhist monk, compiled by Hyŏngnyŏn Chŏng in 1075). *Samdaemok* (compiled in Shilla in 888) was purportedly a large collection of poems, but only the title has survived.

Korea has two poetry traditions, *hanshi* (poems by Korean poets in Chinese characters) and vernacular poems, which are invariably songs. *Hanshi* are to be read and contemplated; the vernacular poetry is to be sung and heard. *Hanshi* aimed at personal cultivation, vernacular poetry at entertainment, although this generalization must not be pushed too far. Personal cultivation should be distinguished from the merely didactic; many *shijo*, for example, were blatantly instructional. Vernacular poetry was composed for the most part against a convivial background of wine, music, and dance; *hanshi* poetry was a much more private discipline. This does not mean

---

1. Kim Hŭnggyu, *Understanding Korean Literature*, translated by Robert J. Fouser, p. 57.

that vernacular poetry was inferior. Good poetry both seeks personal cultivation and entertains. Shilla *hyangga* and Koryŏ *kayo* are perhaps old Korea's finest poetic achievements, a perfect amalgam of cultivation and entertainment.

The following poems have survived from pre-Shilla times.

KONGHUIN (HARP MELODY)

This lyric from Old Chosŏn, translated into Chinese in Haedong yŏksa, *is the oldest Korean poem in the records. The song is also found in an Old Jin dynasty document, however; hence there are doubts about whether it is Chinese or Korean.*

Yŏ Ok composed this song after hearing the harrowing background tale from her ferryman husband. A white-haired crazy man had come to the river that morning. The waves were rough, but the man, unmoved by the pleas of his wife, insisted on crossing and was drowned in the attempt. His wife poured out her sorrow on the harp. Yŏ Ok, moved by her husband's tale, took down her harp and composed "Konghuin."

Don't cross the river, love.
Ah, you dare to cross the river, love.
Swept away, drowned, love.
What am I to do?

HWANGJO KA (SONG OF THE ORIOLES)

Dated 17 BC and translated into Chinese, this poem was recorded in Samguk sagi *(a fifty-volume compendium of all things Korean). This unique source of Korean lore was compiled by Kim Pushik (1075–1151) between 1130 and 1145 at the command of King Injong (1122–1146).*

The kingdom of Koguryŏ (37 BC–AD 668) included Manchuria and most of the Korean peninsula. King Yuri, Koguryŏ's second monarch, went hunting one day. His queens fought in his absence: Zhiji (who was from Han China), at a loss to control her anger, left for home. When Yuri returned from the hunt, he galloped after her but failed to persuade her to return. Resting in the shade of a tree on his way home, he saw orioles flying back and forth and composed this song:

Fluttering orioles
cavort in pairs.
Who will go home
with this lonely man?

This first-century poem, translated into Chinese, was recorded in Samguk yusa *in the section on the foundation myth of Karak kuk. Karak kuk (42?–562) was one of the six kingdoms of Kaya kuk, founded by King Kim Suro and his brothers; it was located along the lower reaches of the Naktong River.*

"Kuji ka" was a petition sung by the people to persuade King Kim Suro to come down to earth.

> Lord turtle, lord turtle,
> stick out your head.
> If you refuse,
> we'll roast and eat you.

POEM PRESENTED TO GENERAL YU ZHONGWEN

This seventh-century, five-character poem is the oldest hanshi *in the records. In 612 General Ŭlchi Mundŏk of Koguryŏ sent this poem to General Yu Zhongwen of Sui. The idea was to lure the general into thinking that he had won.*

> Your god-like strategy had all the brightness of heaven;
> your shrewd ploys exhausted the wisdom of earth.
> You won the battle; your honors are great.
> Contented now, I trust you will desist from war.

HAE KASA (SONG OF THE SEA)

This seventh-century poem, translated into Chinese, was recorded in Samguk yusa, *with the following story. Prince Sunjong, governor of Kangnŭng, was walking along the seashore with Lady Suro, his beautiful wife. Suddenly the Dragon of the East Sea came from the water and abducted Lady Suro. Prince Sunjong was in anguish. An old man passing by reassured the prince: he would tell the local people to sing a song that would secure the release of Lady Suro. This is the song they sang:*

> Turtle, turtle, let Suro go!
> To filch the wife of another is a grievous sin.
> If you persist in your perfidy,
> we'll net and roast you for dinner!

Shilla *Hanshi* (Korean Poems in Chinese)

Chinese characters were introduced early into Korea. "Hwangjo ka" (Song of the Orioles), which is attributed to King Yuri (?–18) and dates back to Koguryŏ, was transcribed in Chinese. The inscription (1,759 characters) on the monument of the Koguryŏ monarch Kwanggaet'o (391–412) is in Chinese, as is General Ŭlchi Mundŏk's poem to the Sui general Yu Zhongwen, written in 612.

In the seventh century Sŏl Ch'ong created the *hyangch'al* writing system, which made possible the transcription of the Korean vernacular in Chinese characters. This cumbersome system was used to transcribe *hyangga*, but it was discontinued in Koryŏ. Subsequently, Korean vernacular verse was either transmitted orally or translated into Chinese. A script to record the vernacular did not come into being until Sejong and his scholar group promulgated *Hunmin chŏng'um* (Right Sounds to Educate the People) in 1446.

Chinese was used extensively in Paekche and Shilla from the fourth century. By the time of Unified Shilla (668–935), it was common for the educated class to write classical Chinese poetry. Kukchagam (forerunner of Sŏnggyun'gwan, the National Confucian Academy) was established in Koryŏ in 930, and the Chinese civil service examination system (*kwagŏ*) was adopted in 958. Classical Chinese became the cornerstone of a good education. Skill in poetic composition was a major indicator of ability to serve in the bureaucracy. It was also a yardstick of literary ability and personal cultivation, which were the way to preferment. The dominance of Chinese as the language of government and literature continued until the end of the nineteenth century, when the rising tide of nationalism led to a rejection of Chinese influence and the promotion of Korea's native script. Sejong's scholars invented the vernacular script in the fifteenth century, but the literati never really accepted it as a cultivated form of expression. It was referred to as *ŏnmun* (vulgar language), fit for those who were deemed unsuited to formal study because of sex, class, or lack of ability. The word *han'gŭl* used today to describe the vernacular script is a twentieth-century coinage.

In *The Art of Chinese Poetry* James Liu enumerates various categories of Chinese verse: four-syllable verse, Old Style, Modern Style, lyric meters, dramatic verse, and dramatic lyrics.[2] All these verse forms were read in Korea, but the vast majority of written *hanshi* were in Old Style (*koch'eshi*) or Modern Style (*shinch'eshi* or *kŭnch'eshi*). Old Style refers to verse in four-, five-, and seven-character lines, which does not follow the rules of tonal parallelism. Modern Style refers to the Tang verse in five- or seven-character lines, which follows the rules of tonal parallelism.

The main divisions of Modern Style are regulated verse (*yulshi*) and the quatrain (*chŏlgu*). A poem in regulated verse has eight lines with five or seven characters, observes tonal parallelism, employs a single rhyme at the end of the second, fourth, sixth, and eighth lines (rhyme at the end of the first line being optional), and shows strict verbal parallelism in the second and third couplets. The quatrain has four lines with five or seven characters, observes tonal parallelism, and employs rhyme at the end of the second and fourth lines (rhyme at the end of the first line being optional).

Regulated verse and the quatrain have a fourfold structure: theme (*ki*), development (*sŭng*), twist or antitheme (*chŏn*), and conclusion (*kyŏl*). This structural profile is deeply imbedded in the minds of Korean commentators: they return to it again and again in discussing not only *hanshi* but also *shijo*, *kasa*, and even contemporary verse.

Regulated verse was so difficult that many Korean poets continued to write Old Style. Precedent for this existed in China, where the great Li Bai used Old Style by choice.

Chinese has four tones that differ from each other in pitch, length, and movement. In determining meter, the first tone is regarded as level (the voice remains on an even keel); the other three are regarded as deflected (the voice moves up or down). *Hanshi* was recited with the Korean pronunciation of the characters. Thus the role of tone in *hanshi* seems to have been very different from the role of tone in Chinese verse. When *hanshi* were recited, the poems would be unintelligible if the listener was not familiar with and could not visualize the characters. Classical Chinese poetry used all the sound resources of the language, including assonance and alliteration. *Hanshi*, however, apparently centered on images or ideas rather than sounds: hence the notion of a poetry to be read and contemplated.

2. James Liu, *The Art of Chinese Poetry*, pp. 20–38.

KIM CHIJANG, 705–803

Kim Chijang was a Shilla prince during the reign of Kyŏngdŏk (742–765). He went to Tang China, where he engaged in ascetic practices on Mount Jiuhua.

SENDING THE NOVICE DOWN THE MOUNTAIN (*hanshi*)

The hermitage was so remote it made you think of home.
Let's part in the house of clouds; you must go down Mount Jiuhua.
Your heart was always on the bamboo terrace, where you played
    horse;
you were careless about collecting gold dust from the gold lode.
There'll be no more calling the moon when filling your bottle in the
    stream;
and there'll be an end to flower games when brewing the tea.
Go in peace; don't cry;
this old monk has mist and twilight for companions.

CH'OE CH'IWŎN, 857–?

Ch'oe Ch'iwŏn was the first Korean poet to achieve an international reputation for his Chinese verse. After passing the Tang civil service examination, he worked for a time as a bureaucrat in China before returning to Shilla and accepting an official post. In his later years he became disillusioned with the corruption endemic in Shilla society. He retired to his hermitage on Kaya san (Mount Kaya), where he pursued a life of study and seclusion. Kaya san is a scenic mountain in the Kyŏngsang area, the site of one of Korea's most famous temples, Haein-sa.

The quality of Ch'oe Ch'iwŏn's imagination is evident in "Beside Mirror Terrace," where he sees a departing boat as a bird disappearing in flight, and in the justly famous "Autumn Night in the Rain," where he demonstrates his loneliness by effectively separating body and spirit.

BESIDE MIRROR TERRACE ON YELLOW MOUNTAIN RIVER (*hanshi*)

Imgyŏngdae (Beside Mirror Terrace) was on the banks of the Hwangsan (Yellow Mountain) River in the lower reaches of the Naktong River in South Kyŏngsang Province.

The river winds through mist shrouded peaks,
houses and mountains face to face in the water.
A solitary boat takes the full breeze; whither is it bound?
Look! A bird flies off and vanishes without trace!

AUTUMN NIGHT IN THE RAIN (*hanshi*)
Autumn winds sing only plaintive songs.
So few people in this world understand me.
It is the third watch; rain splatters the window.
I sit in front of the lamp, my spirit ten thousand *li* away.

NIGHT RAIN AT THE POSTHOUSE (*hanshi*)
Lodged in the hostelry; late autumn rain falling.
The night is still; lamplight glints on the cold window.
I sit in inner turmoil, filled with self-pity,
a veritable monk in contemplation.

WRITTEN IN MY STUDY ON KAYA SAN (*hanshi*)
Water rushes madly between the bundled rocks; the mountain
    seems to roar.
Even at close range human voices are indistinct.
The constant dread of wrangling in my ears
made me ring the mountain with flowing streams.

LEISURELY STROLL BY THE SEA (*hanshi*)
The tide has gone out; I walk the quiet sands.
The setting sun bathes the ridge in evening light.
Spring hues are at odds with the pain in my heart;
they intoxicate me like the flowers of home.

SPRING BREEZE (*hanshi*)
I know you've come across the sea from home.
I sit at my dawn window trying to recite a poem; it's not easy to collect
    my thoughts.
The breeze flutters the study curtain with tender feelings
that speak of home flowers about to bloom.

SPRING DAWN: TAKING A LEISURELY LOOK (*hanshi*)
The wind shifts the clouds dawdling on the ridge;
the sun deceives reluctant snow into melting on the hill.
How can my spring song express the bitterness of my thoughts?
Like the gull on the seashore I'll make a friend of isolation.

PRESENTED TO A MONK LIVING ALONE
IN A MOUNTAIN HERMITAGE (*hanshi*)
There's only the sound of the wind in the pines to trouble the ear.
White clouds are deep in the weave of the grass-roof hut.
More's the pity the people of the world know this road;
footprints sully the moss on the rocks.

OLD INTENT (*hanshi*)
The fox changes easily into a lovely lady;
the wildcat, too, can become a scholar.
Who knew these two animals would become
so bewitchingly human?
Change actually is not hard;
the real problem is cultivating the heart.
If you want to distinguish real from false,
I pray you look at the mirror of the heart.

PRESENTED TO THE HEAD MONK OF
GOLDEN STREAM TEMPLE (*hanshi*)
Kŭmch'ŏn-sa (Golden Stream Temple) in Okchŏn County in North Ch'ungch'ŏng Province was burned to the ground in the Hideyoshi Wars. White Cloud Stream was in Paeg'un (White Cloud) Valley.

You built on the banks of White Cloud Stream;
for thirty years you have been head monk.
With a smile you point to the single road that passes the gate.
At the bottom of the mountain it becomes a thousand tracks!

Shilla *Hyangga*

Hyangga originally meant "songs of our country" or "songs of our village," not—as commonly supposed—to distinguish Korean songs from Chinese songs but because this was the only way of saying "songs of home." The term *hyangga* is used today to refer to the fourteen Shilla poems in *Samguk yusa* and the eleven Koryŏ Buddhist poems in *Kyunyŏ chŏn*. These poems were recorded in *hyangch'al*, a writing system that used Chinese characters for their phonetic or logographic values. *Hyangch'al* was standardized circa 692 by the scholar Sŏl Ch'ong. It should be noted, however, that *hyangga* were originally oral compositions and were only subsequently written down in *hyangch'al*.

The formal study of *hyangga* began with the research of the Japanese scholar Ogura Shimpei (1929) and continued with Yang Chudong's groundbreaking study *Koga yŏn'gu* (1942). Korean scholars have written countless books and articles on the subject. Despite the wealth of material published in the last fifty years, however, the poems have yet to be explicated to everyone's satisfaction. The translations in this volume are based for the most part on the readings of Kim Wanjin in *Hyangga haedokpŏp yŏn'gu* (1980) and Kang Kil'un in *Hyangga shin haedok yŏn'gu* (1995). Kang's book has the added attraction of giving the readings of the principal commentators since Yang Chudong. These alternative readings are reflected from time to time in the translations.

Some points should be noted. First, the body of Shilla *hyangga* is only fourteen poems, a very small number from which to draw general conclusions. Second, the individual poems were written over a period of several hundred years, again making general conclusions difficult. Third, scholars' explications of texts differ widely. Fourth, while eight or nine of the fourteen Shilla *hyangga* have a Buddhist frame of reference, five or six are not necessarily Buddhist in inspiration, and three are arguably Confucian in spirit. While "Anmin ka" is characterized as Confucian in spirit, however, what it says about the relationship between king and subject could equally well be said by any poet in any feudal culture in the world. Though Confucian values can be invoked in the description of the relationship between king and subject in the other two poems, what these poems say about loyalty is universal.

The Shilla *hyangga* were composed sometime between the sixth and the tenth century. They show variety in form: four four-line poems, three eight-line poems, and seven ten-line poems. The literary historians say that the four-line *hyangga* developed from simple folk songs; this four-line form in turn developed into the eight-line *hyangga* and finally into the ten-line *hyangga*. Kim Hŭnggyu notes that "although the three forms of *hyangga* may have developed one from another, they also existed alongside each other as independent forms."[3]

Rhythm, according to the scholars, is determined by breath-groups (1–5 per line) and syllable count (1–7) within each breath-group. The prosodic analysis of *hyangga* leaves much to be desired. In the first place, scholars are not certain how the poems sounded, surely a huge obstacle to the formulation of any prosody. Second, a prosody that allows 1–5 breath-groups per line and 1–7 syllables in each breath group is so elastic that it hardly functions as a norm at all.

Commentators point to shamanist, magical, and incantatory elements as the bedrock of *hyangga* and indeed of the entire Korean poetry tradition. In the context of the accounts that accompany the poems in *Samguk yusa*, this judgment is inevitable; but when the poems are read as independent texts, they present quite a different story. "Ch'ŏyong ka," for example, depicts an adultery. It presents a dilemma but offers no solution. The poem itself contains nothing incantatory or magical. That content comes from the related note in *Samguk yusa*, which says that the seducer is the Fever Spirit and Ch'ŏyong is a mythical figure with magical power to overcome sickness. The Koryŏ *kayo* "Ch'ŏyong ka," which is undoubtedly incantatory, enforces this interpretation. Other poems can be taken as perfectly orthodox expressions of the prayer of petition (heal the child, deliver the land, and so forth).

Interpreting *hyangga* primarily as "primitive" religious songs does them an enormous disservice. These poems are literature; although perhaps uneven in literary quality, they show (to a lesser or greater degree) the spit and polish of achieved poetry. The best of them are superb: sleepless nights in the mugwort wilderness; the old man's gift of flowers to Lady Suro, break-

3. Kim Hŭnggyu, *Understanding Korean Literature*, p. 60.

ing the shackles of conventional response; Shinch'ung's hurt depicted by the ripples in a moonlit pond; brother and sister as scattered leaves from a single tree; Lord Kip'a's nobility expressed in the image of the pine never cowled by snow; the dramatic presentation of Ch'ŏyong's dilemma—"Legs once mine, now purloined." These go far beyond the felicities of a "primitive" religious poetry. This is a fully developed tradition that unfortunately only survives in a very fragmented way.

SŎDONG YO (SŎDONG'S SONG) (*hyangga*)

According to Samguk yusa, *"Sŏdong yo" (Sŏdong's Song), sometimes called "Mattung yo," was composed by Sŏdong (subsequently King Mu of Paekche). He wanted to marry Princess Sŏnhwa, the daughter of King Chinp'yŏng, the twenty-sixth monarch of Shilla. Sŏdong shaved his head and entered the Shilla capital, where he distributed yams (or potatoes) to the children of the city and sang this song. After the song spread throughout the capital, Sŏnhwa was banished from the royal palace. Sŏdong achieved his objective: Sŏnhwa became his wife.*

"Sŏdong yo" existed as a popular folk song long before it was recorded in Samguk yusa. *It is a short dramatic account of a love affair, quite different in terms of feeling from the moral dilemma that* Samguk yusa *presents.*

Princess Sŏnhwa
had marriage on her mind
the night she stole into Mattung's room
and took him in her arms.

HYESŎNG KA (COMET SONG) (*hyangga*)

"Hyesŏng ka" is among the oldest of the hyangga. *It is problematical in terms of both exegesis and the background account in* Samguk yusa.

Samguk yusa *says that a troop of* hwarang *(warrior youths of Shilla) on a trip to the East Coast saw a comet in the sky. This ill omen boded a serious threat to the nation, so the three* hwarang *hesitated to leave. Master Yungch'ŏn sang this* hyangga, *whereupon the comet disappeared from the sky and the marauding Japanese were driven from the land.*

The accuracy of the Samguk yusa *account is questioned, because no historical document contains corroborating evidence of a Japanese invasion at this time. Many of the major commentators regard the song as incantatory, part of a ritual to drive evil from the land.*

Long, long ago, a mirage was seen over a fortress
on the shores of the Eastern Sea.

"The Japanese army is here," the people cried,
and they lit the signal fire.
Three proud *hwarang* were visiting near.
The moon lit her lamp; the comet swept its path.
"Look, the Japanese comet!" one of the *hwarang* cried.
The comet that followed the moon in rising
followed the moon in setting.

P'UNG YO (SONG OF THE WIND) (*hyangga*)

Much of the discussion of "P'ung yo" (recorded in Samguk yusa*) has centered on whether it is a folk song, a work song, or a Buddhist devotional song. It may have been all three at different stages of its history.*

During the reign of Queen Sŏndŏk of Shilla (632–647), Samguk yusa *notes, many miraculous deeds were ascribed to a skilled artist monk called Yangji. While working on the sixteen-foot Buddha image in Yŏngmyo-sa (Temple of the Holy Shrine), he tried to banish all distracting thoughts from his mind. To help the monk stay recollected, the men and women of Kyŏngju vied in bringing him clay for the statue, singing this song as they worked.*

A number of conclusions can be drawn from the Samguk yusa *account. First, it is the only indication of Yangji involvement. Second, this account calls for "We" as the subject of the opening line; the text itself could equally well support "I" or "They." Third, it is clear that "P'ung yo" had become a work song by the time* Samguk yusa *was compiled. Fourth, the amount of physical labor involved in carrying clay for the sculpture obviously would not have been very great (especially when shared by the men and women of Kyŏngju), surely an indication of the devotional nature of the song.*

We're here, we're here, we're here, we're here.
People in distress.
So many people in distress;
we're here to gain merit.

KWANŬM KA (SONG TO THE GODDESS OF MERCY) (*hyangga*)

According to Samguk yusa, *Hŭimyŏng, who lived in Han'giri during the reign of Kyŏngdŏk (742–765), brought her blind son to Punhwang-sa (Fragrance and Light Temple). The boy sang this song to the Goddess of Mercy (whose picture adorned the northern wall) and recovered his sight.*

The commentators are divided on whether the song was written by the mother, the five-year-old son, or a third party—possibly a Buddhist nun, whose prayer the child memorized. It could be a popular devotional song, a prayer, or perhaps a ritual incantation.

With or without the Samguk yusa *account, it is difficult to approach the text as anything other than an impassioned prayer of petition.*

On my knees,
hands joined,
I lift my voice in prayer
to the Goddess of Mercy.
I beseech thee:
with one of your thousand hands
take one of your thousand eyes
and bestow it on your suppliant
who is blind.
Ah, ah, in your boundless compassion
hear my prayer.

MO CHUKCHI RANG KA (SONG IN PRAISE OF LORD CHUKCHI)
(*hyangga*)

Samguk yusa *says that "Mo Chukchi rang ka" (also called "Tŭgo kok") was composed by Tŭgo during the reign of the Shilla king Hyoso (692–702). The poet praises his commander Chukchi, minister of state under four monarchs and one of the bravest of the Shilla hwarang. Chukchi served under General Kim Yushin and contributed to the unification of the land.*

Commentators argue about whether the poem is a lament or a song of praise. In the scenario in which the hero is dead, death is the absence that causes the speaker to wrestle with melancholy. The speaker's longing drives him to sleepless nights on the road as he searches out the hero's grave. In the song of praise scenario, physical separation leads the speaker to melancholy, and reflection on the aging process leads to sadness. The speaker's sense of personal devastation is so great that he finds himself wandering in the mugwort wilderness. The translation supports either interpretation.

Past springs return no more:
absence makes me wrestle with melancholy.
The face that illumined the palace
is furrowed and worn.
If only we could be together,
even for the briefest moment!
My Lord, longing drives me to the road:
to sleepless nights in the mugwort wilderness.

HŎNHWA KA (PRESENTING THE FLOWERS) (*hyangga*)

Samguk yusa *tells us that King Sŏngdŏk (r. 702–737) appointed Prince Sunjong of Shilla as magistrate of Kangnŭng. Sunjong left to take up his post, accompanied by Lady Suro, his beautiful wife. The official party came to a high cliff crowned by azaleas in full bloom. Lady Suro expressed a desire to have some of the azalea blooms, but her entourage ignored her. An old man leading a cow who happened to be passing heard her request and promptly climbed the cliff to get her the flowers. "Hŏnhwa ka" was his song.*

"Hŏnhwa ka" does not pose serious textual problems. Despite some minor problems (such as the exact shade of red in the opening line), overall the scholars agree on the explication of the text. The problems begin with the interpretation of the poem. The critics treat it variously as a worldly song of human desire, a shamanist incantatory song, a song associated with Buddhist ascetic practices, and a song of a god or man-god.

Allow me to tether my cow
beneath the red rock.
Be not embarrassed by what I do:
I'll cut the azaleas and present them to you.

WŎN KA (SONG OF A BITTER HEART) (*hyangga*)

Samguk yusa *records that King Hyosŏng (r. 737–742), while he was still crown prince, played* paduk *(a popular board game) with Shinch'ung under a pine tree. The prince promised never to forget Shinch'ung: he would turn into the old pine, he said, if he forgot. Shortly afterward the young prince became king and promptly forgot his friend. Shinch'ung put his pain into a song. He stuck this song to the old pine, which immediately died. Hyosŏng ordered an investigation into the death of the tree, and this led to the discovery of the poem. The king remembered his promise, summoned his old friend, and granted him a title and a stipend. The pine was miraculously restored.*

The scholars contest the meaning of every line of "Wŏn ka." In purely poetic terms, however, Kim Wanjin's version is by far the most compelling. The poem opens with a fine image of unchanging love, the evergreen pine, then moves quickly to a complaint over changed affections. The beloved is the moon, and the endless ripples in the pond express the hurt in the speaker's heart. He wants to see the beloved, but "the world" makes meeting impossible.

The great spreading pine
ignores the exigencies of autumn.
You said you would emulate that tree,
but the face that I loved changed.
Again and again I feel the hurt:

[15

ripples in a moonlit pond.
I want to see you,
but the world decrees parting.

TOSOL KA (SONG OF THE TSITA HEAVEN) (*hyangga*)

Samguk yusa *records that in the nineteenth year of the reign of Kyŏngdŏk (760) two suns appeared in the sky, an omen of imminent catastrophe. The royal astrologer suggested that a monk be found to compose and recite a prayer, "Hŏnhwa kongdŏk" (The Virtue of Strewing the Flowers), to ward off the danger. The king had an altar built in front of his audience hall (Chowŏn chŏn) and then went to a pavilion (Ch'ŏngyang nu) to await the arrival of a propitious monk.*

A monk named Wŏlmyŏng (Bright Moon, literally Moon Bright), who happened to be passing the palace, was quickly brought into the king's presence and commissioned to compose a prayer. Wŏlmyŏng said that he would compose a hyangga *because he was not well versed in Sanskrit. The king agreed, and Wŏlmyŏng composed "Tosol ka." Soon afterward the mysterious second sun disappeared. The king was delighted and rewarded Wŏlmyŏng.*

It is very difficult to make any connection between the poem and the mysterious astrological phenomena that are supposed to have been its occasion. The poem seems like a simple but lovely prayer: the speaker asks the flowers to do what they do best, embody beauty, in the service of Maitreya, presumably in the hope that Maitreya will return the favor to humankind.

Today I sing "Strewing the Flowers."
Scattered petals,
attend to the command of an honest heart:
serve the smiling Maitreya!

CHE MANGMAE KA (RITUAL SERVICE FOR A DEAD SISTER) (*hyangga*)

Samguk yusa *records that Wŏlmyŏng made a ritual offering to the spirit of his dead sister and composed the following song. As he sang his song, a mad wind arose and blew away the paper money used in the ritual.*

Traditionally, commentators view this poem as an effort to sublimate in religious terms the fear of death and the feelings of loss arising from the death of a sister. The images of leaves and branches representing the family relationship and the mad wind representing the affairs of the world not only give death's tragedy more impact but also add a dimension to the monk's prayer for transcendence. The poem has lovely touches everywhere: the abruptness of death's call, giving no consideration to the human need to say good-bye; the ephemeral nature of life: leaves on a tree, scattered who knows where. The monk has only his faith to sustain him. He must continue with the task of self-cultivation until he meets his sister in paradise. The poem involves paradox too: the transcendent monk should be above all desire, including the desire to meet his sister in the afterlife. Perhaps the point is that there is no complete transcendence of the human condition.

You left
on the life-death road,
with no word
of farewell:
we are two leaves, torn
by early autumn winds
from a single tree,
scattered who knows where.
Let me abide in the Way, I pray,
until we meet in the Western Paradise.

ANMIN KA (APPEASING THE PEOPLE) (*hyangga*)

According to Samguk yusa, *King Kyŏngdŏk (r. 742–765) complimented the monk Ch'ungdam on his beautiful song about Lord Kip'a and asked him to compose a song on the theme of a peaceful reign. Ch'ungdam composed "Anmin ka."* Samguk yusa *says that Kyŏngdŏk was greatly pleased with Ch'ungdam's composition. Exactly what the king found so delightful is not clear. "Anmin ka" is the least distinguished of the* hyangga.

Cho Tongil suggests that Kyŏngdŏk lacked an heir and was under severe political pressure when he commissioned the song. Samguk yusa *does not mention this. The gist of the relevant passage is that Kyŏngdŏk was having problems producing an heir and commissioned a monk to intercede for him in heaven. The monk said that a daughter was possible but not a son. The king refused to accept the will of heaven and sent the monk back again. Eventually the king was given a son who was effeminate in character and proved to be a disaster on the throne.*

The king is father;
each minister is loving mother;
the people are foolish children—
thus the people come to know love.
The people live in grinding poverty:
feed them, guide them.
They won't ever leave;

they will know the land is governed well.
When king, ministers, and people all do their part
the land knows a great peace.

CH'AN KIP'A RANG KA (SONG IN PRAISE OF LORD KIP'A) (*hyangga*)

Ch'ungdam the monk has the distinction of having written the least distinguished and the most distinguished of the hyangga. "Ch'an Kip'a rang ka" more than compensates for the weakness of "Anmin ka"; it is a superb poem by any standard. The great disparity between the versions of the leading commentators should be noted, however.

Samguk yusa gives no context for this poem. The commentators readily make up for this uncharacteristic skimpiness, offering a rich array of extraneous speculation. It is a poem in praise of Kip'a, a legendary character in Buddhist scripture who is the ideal Shilla man; or a prayer for the future son of King Kyŏngdŏk; or a poem in praise of the providence of the Lord of Heaven. Lee Ŏryŏng notes that the word kip'a appears regularly in Buddhist scriptures, where it is associated with eternal life. Kip'a is thus a symbol of transcendence. The strength of the poem rests in the embodiment of a noble theme in two fine images. First, the image of Lord Kip'a's face mirrored in the brightness of the Milky Way and his mind reflected in the bed of the stream; and second, Lord Kip'a's demeanor, expressed in the image of the pine tree never covered by winter snow. Moonlight is everywhere in the poem, with concomitant feelings of brightness, loneliness, and creativity: it chases away the white clouds (human desire in the mundane world), lights up the bed of the stream, and presumably illuminates the branches of the pine. In the process, it illuminates Kip'a. As a poem of transcendence, this poem is unequaled in the history of Korean literature. Kip'a is depicted as a man of cosmic proportions, bright in soul as the Milky Way, who links heaven and earth like the great pine on the mountain.

I'm worn out by tears.
The dew-sparkling moon
chases away
white clouds.
Your face shines
in the blue of the Milky Way;
I seek your mirrored mind
among the pebbles lining the stream.
You are like the top branches of the pine,
never cowled by winter snow.

WŎN WANGSAENG KA (SONG IN SEARCH OF ETERNAL LIFE)
(*hyangga*)

Samguk yusa *notes that in the reign of King Munmu (661–681) two close friends,
Kwangdŏk and Ŏmjang, immersed themselves in Buddhist ascetic practices. They had an
agreement that the one who was called first to paradise would tell the other of his imminent
going. One day Ŏmjang heard a voice, saying: I am going to paradise; follow me when your
time comes. The next day, Ŏmjang went to Kwangdŏk's house; his friend was indeed dead.*

*After the funeral, Ŏmjang suggested to Kwangdŏk's wife that they live together. She
agreed; but when Ŏmjang attempted to share her bed, she cried that in ten years of
marriage to Kwangdŏk she had never shared her flesh. Chastened and filled with regret,
Ŏmjang sought out the great priest Wŏnhyo to cultivate his heart and learn the road to
salvation.*

*Commentators are divided about the narrator of the poem. Is it the voice of Kwangdŏk
as he journeys to the Pure Land; of Kwangdŏk's wife, also prepared to make the journey; of
Ŏmjang, chastened, repentant, and resolved to mortify his flesh so that he too may journey
to the Pure Land; of the great monk Wŏnhyo, telling his people how the Pure Land can be
attained; or, finally, of a fervent Buddhist believer? The pros and cons have been argued for
years, and we are no nearer the truth. The translation supports all these approaches. This
is the poem of a man or woman engaged in ascetic practice, a suppliant of extraordinary
sincerity and dedication who realizes that mortification of the flesh is at the heart of self-
cultivation. Moonlight fills the poem, as it so often fills the best* hyangga. *The moon here
presumably lights the way for the "bright-hearted" on the journey to the Western Paradise.*

Moon,
are you westering?
Pray to Amithaba.
Say
there is one
who worships the judicial throne,
who, hands joined in prayer,
longs for the Pure Land.
Let the forty-eight vows be kept,
let the flesh be annihilated;
let me enter the Pure Land.

UJŎK KA (MEETING WITH BANDITS) (*hyangga*)

Samguk yusa *tells us that Yŏngjae was a Shilla monk famous for his humor and his ability to sing* hyangga. *In the twilight of his life he decided to go to Chiri san (Mount Chiri) to spend the rest of his life in ascetic practices. On his way to Chiri san, bandits rushed upon him from the forest, brandishing their swords. Yŏngjae, not at all frightened, praised the artistic excellence of their sword dance. The bandits were amazed by his imperturbability in the face of death. They recognized him as the famous singing monk and asked for a song. He sang "Ujŏk ka." The bandits were so impressed that they offered him two rolls of silk. He declined the gift, saying that fine goods and bribes are the way to perdition. Ashamed of their conduct, the bandits threw down their weapons, followed Yŏngjae into the mountains, and became monks.*

The text of "Ujŏk ka" is very problematical. Some characters are missing in the original in Samguk yusa, *and explications of the text are very diverse. The translation is a composite of various readings.*

> Ignorant of my true self,
> I wandered in the depths;
> now I break like a bird from the net,
> searching for the world of Bodhi.
> Confronted by my bandit lord,
> am I to turn aside in fear?
> Death by the sword
> means the bright land for me;
> but it is not much of a merit hill
> to build a mansion on.

CH'ŎYONG KA (CH'ŎYONG'S SONG) (hyangga)

Samguk yusa *reports that the reign of Hŏn'gang (875–886) was a time of soft music and sweet rain. One day the king went on a picnic to Kaeunp'o (Port of the Clearing of the Clouds, modern Ulsan). On the seashore he found himself enveloped in mist. The royal astrologer assured him that this was the Dragon of the East Sea at play. To placate the dragon, the king issued a decree ordering the construction of a pagoda; the mist lifted immediately.*

When the king returned to the capital, he was accompanied by one of the sons of the dragon. The king named him Ch'ŏyong and gave him high rank and a beautiful wife. Ch'ŏyong's wife attracted the attentions of the Fever Spirit, who seduced her. Ch'ŏyong returned one night to find his wife in a compromising situation. His response was to sing this song, dance, and turn away. The Fever Spirit was so impressed that he announced he would never enter a house where Ch'ŏyong's portrait was hanging. Subsequently, the people hung Ch'ŏyong's portrait in their houses as a protection against disease.

The commentators are agreed in the main about the exegesis of the text, though the final line remains somewhat problematical. "How could he do it?" has been suggested as an alternative reading. Most commentators, however, follow the original exegesis—"what am I to do?"—though opinions differ on whether this constitutes a negative or a positive stance.

The central question remains: what weight is to be given to the Samguk yusa account? Is the poem to be seen as incantatory, part of a shamanist rite? Is Ch'ŏyong a mythical figure with magical power to overcome sickness; is the seducer the Fever Spirit? Or is the poem to be approached as an independent text, in which case Ch'ŏyong presents the adultery scene as a moral dilemma? In poetic terms, this scenario is much more attractive. Ch'ŏyong may not resolve the dilemma in the ambiguous last line, but he does leave the way open for resolution. Transcendence is one solution; ignoring the situation is another.

> I reveled all night
> in the moonlit capital,
> came home and discovered
> four legs in my bed!
> Two are mine;
> whose are the other two?
> Legs once mine, now purloined,
> what am I to do?

Koryŏ *Kayo*

The vernacular poems of late Koryŏ (after the military coup of 1170) are known as Koryŏ *kayo* (*sog'yo*). The term is a convenient general term for various lyrics, including folk songs, court dance music adapted from folk songs, Buddhist songs, and shaman chants. These songs were love songs for the most part, earthy, lovely, and sexy as only folk songs can be. The earlier Shilla *hyangga* were recorded in *hyangch'al*, a cumbersome writing system that used Chinese characters to record Korean sounds. The Koryŏ songs, however, were transmitted orally. They were only recorded after Sejong and his team of scholars invented a vernacular script in the fifteenth century.

Koryŏ *kayo* came down to us by a complex route. Initially popular among the people, they were introduced into the fun-loving Koryŏ court, where they enjoyed even greater popularity. From Koryŏ they passed to Chosŏn, where court musicians set them to *a-ak* court music. No one knows to what extent the songs were altered to fit the music and to what extent they were snipped by the scissors of the censors of the Chosŏn court. There is evidence of stanzas added, the suspicion of stanzas deleted. The sentiments expressed in these songs often were not in accord with the Confucian moral norms current in Chosŏn dynasty society. Great scholars from the past (including Yi T'oegye) regarded them as vulgar, not at all the thing to teach children.

The Koryŏ *kayo* that survived are not a representative selection of the poems of this period. Only songs that were popular survived: ritual songs, songs of love, songs of betrayal. This poetry is narrow in scope but close to the world of everyday consequences—where men and women are wary of the gods, where they love and hate, where they abandon and are abandoned, and where passion and feeling are on the fingertips, not hidden under the blanket of Confucian precept. Unfortunately, it is impossible to say whether surviving Koryŏ *kayo* represent what these songs originally were. Most of them cannot be dated; nor can the poets be named.

There are three sources for Koryŏ *kayo*: *Akhak kwebŏm* (Canon of Music), *Akchang kasa* (Music and Lyrics), and *Shiyong hyangakpo* (Contemporary Music Scores). All three date from the Chosŏn dynasty.

Akhak kwebŏm, compiled and edited in 1493 by order of Sŏngjong, was a complete guide: music, lyrics, dance, illustrations. Unfortunately, it disappeared during the Hideyoshi Wars (1592–1598). It was reissued in 1610 during the reign of Kwanghaegun, with Yi Chŏnggu, among others, in charge of the project. This reissue is in the National Archives (Kyujanggak). It was photocopied for the first time in 1933. A copy of *Akhak kwebŏm* survives in Japan, taken there sometime during the Hideyoshi Wars. This is the only pre-Hideyoshi copy extant and is surmised to be a copy of the original. *Akhak kwebŏm* contains four Koryŏ songs: "Tongdong," "Chŏngŭp sa," "Ch'ŏyong ka," and "Chŏng Kwajŏng kok." It also contains some other songs, but they either are in *hanmun* (Chinese characters) or were composed in the Chosŏn era.

Akchang kasa is thought to have been edited by Pak Chun during the Chungjong-Myŏngjong era (sixteenth century), but the author and date cannot be determined with accuracy. Only one copy survives, and it is clearly post-Hideyoshi. The book contains twenty-four songs, of which ten are Koryŏ songs; the rest are either *hanmun* compositions or songs composed in the Chosŏn era. The Koryŏ songs are "Chŏngsŏk ka," "Ch'ŏngsan pyŏlgok," "Sŏ'gyŏng pyŏlgok," "Samo kok," "Ssanghwa chŏm," "Isang kok," "Kashiri," "Hallim pyŏlgok," "Manjŏn ch'un," and "Ch'ŏyong ka."

Shiyong hyangakpo is a comprehensive survey of native music from Koryŏ to early Chosŏn; the editor and date are unknown. Judging from paper, ink, and other internal evidence, however, the book was presumably written in the time of Chungjong-Myŏngjong or perhaps Sŏnjo (sixteenth and early seventeenth century). Part of the collection of Yi Kyŏmno, it was photocopied in 1954 and introduced to the academic world. The book contains twenty-six songs, of which sixteen were hitherto unknown. Thirteen of these songs are in Korean and have come down from Koryŏ or earlier. Signs indicate that the songs were touched up or revised in Chosŏn, but they are regarded as native Korean songs. Of the remaining three, "Hwaengsalmun" and "Saengga yoryŏng" are odes in praise of the foundation of Chosŏn and are in *hanmun*, while "Kwiho kok" is "Kashiri" under a different title. "Kunma taewang," "Kuch'ŏn," and "Pyŏl taewang" are all in *ri-ra* nonsense syllables and are presumed to be incantatory. The present volume provides translations for four of these new songs: "Narye ka," "Yugu kok," "Sangjŏ ka," and "Taewang pan." It does not provide translations for "Songhwang pan," "Naedang," and "Taeguk 1, 2, 3."

Commentators discuss the form of Koryŏ *kayo* in the usual breath-group mode. They distinguish two types.

Type 1 has three or four breath-groups per line, with two, three, or four syllables per breath-group (but three most common). Each stanza features a refrain either in the middle or at the end, with no set number of stanzas.

Type 2 has three or four breath-groups per line (but four most common), with two, three, or four syllables per breath-group (but four most common). It has no set number of stanzas.

The prosodic analysis of the Koryŏ *kayo* leaves much to be desired. Analysis is for the most part a numbers game, with no discussion of how different arrangements of syllable and/or breath-group contribute to the making of the poem. These patterns seem to be no more than the natural rhythms of the Korean language.

CHŎNG KWAJŎNG KOK (CHŎNG KWAJŎNG'S SONG)

"Chŏng Kwajŏng kok" (recorded in Akhak kwebŏm*) is unique among the Koryŏ* kayo *in that the author and approximate date of composition are known. The song was written by Chŏng Sŏ (pen name Kwajŏng) circa 1160. He was a relative of Injong and enjoyed the king's personal friendship. When Ŭijong came to the throne, however, Chŏng Sŏ got caught in the skirmishing for power within the court. As a result he was sent into exile. Although the king assured him that he believed him innocent of all charges and promised to work for his swift return to the capital, the call back from exile was not forthcoming. The poem sings of Chŏng Sŏ's sense of personal hurt and abandonment. Commentators traditionally emphasize the poet's undying loyalty to the king, but the poem seems more concerned with the poet's predicament than with his devotion to the king.*

The strength of "Chŏng Kwajŏng kok" is in the image of waning moon and stars (used to depict the poet's situation) and in the ambiguity of the king's attitude. The king has promised to work for an immediate recall, but nothing happens. Is this because the king is powerless in his own court against the machinations of powerful retainers, or is the king so caught up in state affairs that he forgets about the plight of a friend? Either way Chŏng Sŏ's situation is desperate.

In tears I long for my love:
the mountain cuckoo shares my grief.
Only the remnant moon and the stars at first light
know these charges are false.
Would that my soul at least could be with my love.

Who was the transgressor?
Neither blame nor fault accrues, you said.
Words to console.
My heart constricts. Ah, ah,
have you forgotten me already, love?
Love, turn to me, listen to me. Love me.

CHŎNGŬP SA (SONG OF CHŎNGŬP)

"Chŏngŭp sa" is said to date from Paekche (18 BC–AD 660), though scholars today question this. Transmitted orally to Koryŏ and Chosŏn, it is recorded in Akhak kwebŏm. *The song was labeled "immoral" in the reign of Chungjong (1506–1544), a too frank account of relations between the sexes. Obviously a love song, it is reminiscent of "Sŏgyŏng pyŏlgok," though not so developed. The commentators are divided as to whether Chŏngŭp is simply a place name or whether the Chinese characters spring well (chŏng) and village (ŭp) have a further sexual implication. According to* Koryŏ sa akchi, *Chŏngŭp was a subprefecture of Chŏnju; "Chŏngŭp sa" was sung by a wife waiting for her merchant husband to return. She climbed a rock or a high place to survey the scene and sang her impassioned song. The speaker is clearly a woman who is worried about her man. Time keeps passing, and he does not return. She worries that he may have been tempted by the fleshpots of the marketplace and pleads with the moon to light his way safely home. Her final prayer is that he may unburden himself of anything that might detain him and that the light of love may not go out in her life.*

The poem is filled with the brightness of the moon, which offers a sharp contrast to the darkness attacking the speaker's heart. The moon works at several symbolic levels: it indicates the loneliness of the speaker, but at the same time it shows her refusal to abandon hope. It also indicates the temptation that the bright lights of the town pose to her man. The final "nought but night awaits me here" is not despairing. It says simply: "without you my lights go out," a delightful protestation of love.

Moon,
rise high, rise high in the sky,
shine, shine, far and wide.
O-gi-ya o-gang-jo-ri
i-gi-ya ta-rong-di-ri.
Is my man in the marketplace?
I fear he's mired in a sticky space.
O-gi-ya o-gang-jo-ri.

Unburden yourself of all your gear!
Nought but night awaits me here.
O-gi-ya o-gang-jo-ri
i-gi-ya ta-rong-di-ri.

The author and date of this poem, recorded in Akhak kwebŏm, *are unknown. "Tong-dong" is a Korean poetic genre that describes the twelve months of the year. It was popular in both the Koryŏ and the Chosŏn courts, but performance was discontinued on moral grounds in the reign of Chungjong (1506–1544).*

"Tongdong" is a love song, the lament of a woman abandoned by her lover. Her grief is depicted month by month. The commentators seem to think it was not the work of any single author but was most likely a popular song. The title "Tongdong," taken from the refrain, is variously interpreted as the beat of a drum (tungtung) or as the comic flitting of a man and woman in amorous play. It has been suggested that the lover is dead on the basis of verse seven, where ritual offerings are made to the dead, and verse eight, which says that Ch'usŏk (Korea's great harvest festival) without the beloved is not a festival at all. Such a restricted interpretation radically changes the dramatic content of the poem and the quality of the grief expressed. Verses seven and eight, in fact, can be explained easily in terms of annual customs.

The poem opens with an invocation, a prayer for virtue and blessings, followed by a stanza for each month of the year, describing the woman's grievous situation. The first month, winter's end, presents images of her loneliness; streams freeze and thaw in turn, indicating alternating hope and despair. The moon of the second month illuminates the world. Is there any light for her? Azaleas flower in spring, season of new beginnings. What does spring have in store for her? The fourth month comes; the orioles return. Nature follows its accustomed pattern. Why is her love an exception? The fifth month brings Tano Day, one of the major festivals in the lunar calendar. Though her heart is grieving, she offers her love traditional medicaments, wishing him health and long life. The sixth month recalls the old Shilla custom of women throwing away the comb (a symbol of abandoned love) after a ritual washing of the hair. The woman still insists on following her love, in the hope he may look back. In the seventh month she performs the ritual offerings to the dead. Her heart desires to be united with her love forever in the other world. The eight month is the month of Ch'usŏk. No festival is a celebration for her in the absence of her love. The chrysanthemums of the ninth month are put in the wine. The idea presumably is the assuagement of grief through wine. The lime tree of the tenth month poses some interpretive problems. One possible approach is to take the tree as a symbol of beauty. Once it is cut, no one values it. The woman sees herself as a cut tree, doomed to lose the affection of her beloved. In the eleventh month she laments the loneliness of her life. The twelfth month highlights the difficulty of the abandoned woman's lot. The entire poem has been leading to this. Circumstances could occur in which another man would take up her beloved's chopsticks! Is this a threat or a statement of inevitable fact? It is impossible to say.

No other work in the history of Korean poetry is like this poem. This is poetry drama at its best: an abandoned woman examining her situation, reacting passionately to glimmers of hope and intimations of despair, proclaiming her undying love, and unfolding a grieving, betrayed heart. All the skills of the poetic process are here: images used in the cultural context of the traditional year to depict the two faces of the coin of love and the multiple facets of the woman's emotion. Love waxes and wanes through the progression of the seasons. The poem and the woman's feelings build gradually to the climax of the twelfth month, mid-winter, where she announces her dilemma: will she take another man, or will she stay true to "lost" love?

Virtue I offer to the spirits,
blessings I offer to my love.
Come and offer
virtue and blessings.
Ah, ah tong-dong-da-ri.

First month streams
freeze and thaw by turn.
Born into the world,
I'm doomed to live alone.
Ah, ah tong-dong-da-ri.

Second month, full moon:
lantern
brightly hung on high,
you shine on all the people.
Ah, ah tong-dong-da-ri.

Third month, last days; already
azaleas fill the mountain:
born with a beauty
the world will envy.
Ah, ah tong-dong-da-ri.

Fourth month: the orioles
never forget to visit.
Why, why, my ranking love,
do you forget the days of old?
Ah, ah tong-dong-da-ri.

Fifth month, fifth day:
I offer you
Tano morning medicaments:
may you live a thousand years.
Ah, ah tong-dong-da-ri.

Sixth month, full moon.
I follow a while
the comb cast from the cliff,
in the hope my love will look back.
Ah, ah tong-dong-da-ri.

Seventh month, full moon:
I lay out offerings for the dead.
I offer my prayer:
may my love and I go together.
Ah, ah tong-dong-da-ri.

Eight month, full moon:
it is the Ch'usŏk Harvest Festival.
Only with my love
is it a festive day for me.
Ah, ah tong-dong-da-ri.

Ninth month, ninth day:
the yellow chrysanthemums bloom within:
they are for medicinal purposes;
time makes everything indistinct.
Ah, ah tong-dong-da-ri.

Tenth month.
A lime tree chopped in pieces.
My love will not treasure

a cut tree.
Ah, ah tong-dong-da-ri.

Eleventh month: I lie
on a dirt floor, hemp my bedcover.
Burning sorrow is my lot,
divided from my lovely love.
Ah, ah tong-dong-da-ri.

Twelfth month. Chopsticks
cut from pepperwood, laid on a tray,
at an angle for my love.
A stranger puts them to his lips.
Ah, ah tong-dong-da-ri.

CH'ŎYONG KA (CH'ŎYONG'S SONG)

This poem (author and date unknown) is recorded in Akhak kwebŏm. Samguk yusa
says that Hŏn'gang (875–886) went on a picnic on the seashore and found himself en-
veloped in mist. Told by the royal astrologer that this was the Dragon of the East Sea at
play, the king ordered the construction of a pagoda in honor of the dragon. The mist lifted
immediately.

One of the sons of the dragon accompanied the king when he returned to the capital.
The king named him Ch'ŏyong and awarded him high rank and a lovely wife. Ch'ŏyong
returned one night to find his wife in bed with the Fever Spirit. He responded by singing a
song, dancing, and turning away. Impressed, the Fever Spirit said that he would never en-
ter a house displaying Ch'ŏyong's portrait. The people thereafter hung his portrait in their
homes as a protection against disease. In Koryŏ times the Ch'ŏyong myth was incorporated
into various court exorcist rituals. It achieved its ultimate form in Chosŏn. After the for-
mal rite of exorcism on New Year's Eve, the Ch'ŏyong dance was performed twice as a dra-
matic expression of the driving away of sickness.

"Ch'ŏyong ka" begins with a statement of Ch'ŏyong's incantatory power: he dispelled
the three calamities and the eight disasters. Rahu, to whom peace in heaven and earth
is attributed, was a demon in Hindu myth who caused eclipses by swallowing the sun and
the moon.

The second section is a fine description of the mien of Ch'ŏyong, regaled for the rite of
exorcism—perhaps the finest character description in all classical Korean poetry. Ch'ŏyong
is wearing the exorcist mask. The question is asked: Who made the mask? A third-person

narrator describes Ch'ŏyong and says that the people made his mask. From here on, the interpretation of the poem is problematical. An ambiguous reference to cherry, plum, and wild pear is followed by a command to tie Ch'ŏyong's sandal straps (with some dispute about who gives the command to whom). The most satisfactory interpretation of the passage sees cherry, plum, and pear as fever spots on the face of the sick and the tying of the sandal straps as a command to the Fever Spirit to depart. Some connecting phrases have been added in the translation to make this content clear. Ch'ŏyong describes the horror of the adultery scene. The Fever Spirit is warned to flee lest Ch'ŏyong catch him. Ch'ŏyong is told that his role is not to provide gold and treasure but to expel the Fever Spirit. Again problems arise regarding who is speaking to whom. In the Korean, Ch'ŏyong could also be the speaker, in which case the sense would be that he is offered money to do the exorcism. Finally, the Fever Spirit decides to flee. It is interesting that the speaker at the end gives the Fever Spirit the honorific form. In old Korea you could never be too careful!

In the glory days of Shilla
when peace, by Rahu's favor, prevailed in heaven and earth,
Father Ch'ŏyong—
    he said not a word,
    he said not a word—
dispelled in cluster the three calamities, the eight disasters.

Ah, the mien of the man, the mien of Father Ch'ŏyong:
head crowned with flowers,
inclined with the greatest difficulty;
ah, long-lived, broad-browed;
eyebrows thick as mountain foliage;
eyes gentle, full
when trained on someone he loves;
ears crinkly when wind fills the yard;
face pink as pink peach blossoms;
nose high from the five-scent tree;
broad lips worth a thousand pieces of gold;
teeth white as glassy jade;
jutting jaw, praise of many, badge of blessings;
shoulders weighed by *ch'ilbo* treasures,[4]
sleeves hanging loose in joy and celebration;

4. Literally, seven treasures; a form of decorative metalwork.

noble breast, repository of wisdom;
belly full, replete with blessings and knowledge;
hips swaying to rhythms of delight;
long legs share his joy and peace,
broad feet match the dance.

Who made this image of Father Ch'ŏyong?
No needle or thread, no needle or thread,
who made this image of Father Ch'ŏyong?
Many, many people,
the twelve kingdoms combined
to create Father Ch'ŏyong;
yes, many, many people.

The fever spots its victims—cherry, plum, wild pear.
Come quickly; tie my sandal straps; prepare to leave this place.
Straps untied, an imprecation may out.
I reveled late into the night
in Kyŏngju
under the bright moon,
came home and discovered
four legs in my bed.
Ah, two are mine, but whose are the other two?
Fever Spirit,
if Father Ch'ŏyong spots you here,
for certain you are doomed.
Father Ch'ŏyong, treasure and a thousand pieces of gold,
Father Ch'ŏyong, treasure and a thousand pieces of gold,
is that what we require? Not so:
forget the gold, forget the treasure,
drive the Fever Spirit out.
Through mountain and field, for a thousand *li*,
I must avoid Father Ch'ŏyong.
Ah, this is the prayer of the Fever Spirit!

SŎ'GYŎNG PYŎLGOK (SONG OF P'YŎNGYANG)
This poem (author and date unknown) is recorded in Akchang kasa. *It belongs to the
genre of* pyŏlgok, *an unrhymed poem quite distinct from the Chinese mode. The poem is*

thought to have enjoyed great popularity in Koryŏ. It is documented as one of the "vulgar" songs that caught the censor's eye in the Chosŏn court and may have felt the nip of the official scissors.

"Sŏ'gyŏng pyŏlgok" is the song of a woman in love. She likes her life in the capital, but she is willing to leave the security of the capital for a man's love. The poem presents a lovely opposition between the claims of a settled peaceful life in the city and the excitement of pursuing the storms of love in a passionate relationship. It is filled with movement: the woman's willingness to leave P'yŏngyang, the flowing river, the boatman picking up passengers, the beloved about to embark. Movement reflects not just life's journey but also the constant movements of the heart: love and hate, joy and sorrow, serenity and anxiety. The certainty of the woman's love stands in sharp contrast to the uncertainty of the man's pledge. This is an archetypical theme. She says her love is so strong that she will not break faith, even if she is left alone for a thousand years.

All, however, is not well. Note how tentative the love bond is throughout. She never claims that the man she loves has proclaimed his love for her. In fact, at this juncture, the beloved does not even seem to be listening. Already he is on the boat bound for the other side of the Taedong. In desperation, she turns her attention to the boatman. Does he not know, she asks, the sexual needs of his own wife? How can he take her man away? Then, almost by accident, she gets to her ultimate fear—rival flowers growing in profusion on the other side of the river: if her man goes, he will pluck those flowers! Husband or sweetheart, who knows?

Is this the original as it was transmitted from Koryŏ to the musicians of the Chosŏn court or has it been doctored? It is impossible to say. The string of pearls image occurs elsewhere in Koryŏ poetry; it may have been added. It smells a little of artifice in a poem where everything else is simple and fresh. This is not a song that persuades with cold logic. The feelings here are universal, elemental: their tug is at the heart not the head; their vehicle is a rueful smile.

"Sŏ'gyŏng pyŏlgok" makes its music through repetition and the use of a double refrain. The first line of each stanza consists of a phrase followed by a three-syllable refrain, a-jul-ga. The opening phrase is repeated in the second line, which is followed by a second refrain, wi tu-ŏ-rŏng-shyŏng ta-rang-di-ri, a mouthful for any would-be translator. The refrains are fillers to match the music; they do not have semantic meaning. The translation drops the first refrain and employs a single-stress first line followed by a three-stress second line and a three-stress refrain manufactured for the purpose, using some but not all of the original syllables.

P'yŏngyang,
P'yŏngyang, our first town.
Wi-ta-ring-di-ri.

Peaceful,
peaceful, the rebuilt fort.
Wi-ta-ring-di-ri.

I choose,
I choose, to leave the loom.
Wi-ta-ring-di-ri.

Love me,
love me, I'll follow in tears.
Wi-ta-ring-di-ri.

The pearls,
the pearls, they drop on the rock.
Wi-ta-ring-di-ri.

The string,
the string, will the pearl-string snap?
Wi-ta-ring-di-ri.

Alone,
alone, for a thousand years.
Wi-ta-ring-di-ri.

My faith,
my faith, will it disintegrate?
Wi-ta-ring-di-ri.

How broad,
how broad, the Taedong River!
Wi-ta-ring-di-ri.

Boatman,
boatman, why do you sail?
Wi-ta-ring-di-ri.

Your wife,
your wife, don't you know what she craves?
Wi-ta-ring-di-ri.

You don't,
you don't, so you take my man.
Wi-ta-ring-di-ri.

Across,
across, sweet flowers bloom.
Wi-ta-ring-di-ri.

If he goes,
if he goes, he'll pluck those buds.
Wi-ta-ring-di-ri.

CH'ŎNGSAN PYŎLGOK (SONG OF THE GREEN MOUNTAIN)

"Ch'ŏngsan pyŏlgok" (author and date unknown) is recorded in Akchang kasa *but is not mentioned in* Koryŏ sa; *hence it cannot be affirmed definitely that it is a Koryŏ song. Its form and content are different from the songs of Chosŏn, however, with similarities to "Sŏ'gyŏng pyŏlgok" and "Hallim pyŏlgok" in terms of form, imagery, and sentiment that account for it being treated traditionally as a Koryŏ song.*

Theories on the social status and predicament of the speaker vary. One reading sees the speaker as a nobleman, fallen in grace politically or perhaps hiding his rank. This nobleman narrator, writing about the misery of ordinary people in the face of calamity within and outside the kingdom, expresses his longing for better times in the symbols of mountain and sea. Another reading sees the speaker as a poor farmer who expresses his grief at being robbed of his land by the ruling elite and at being reduced to the life of a wanderer. Other readings posit a number of speakers, involved in political crises of various kinds (uprisings, purges, slave revolts). Some commentators place these crises at the end of Koryŏ, while others say that they were a direct result of the Mongol Invasion (ca. 1250). One crucial piece of external evidence is that the song was banned in the Chosŏn court. Songs were presumably banned for moral or political reasons. This one must have been politically unacceptable.

The third stanza poses two major problems. The first is the conflict of tense in the opening line between "do you see" and "the bird that flew [or was flying, used to fly]." How can one see something when the action is already finished? "Do you see the bird that flew" only makes sense if the bird is now back in sight. The choice in English is to say "Did you see the bird that flew?" or *"Did you see the bird flying?"* or *"Do you see the bird that is flying?"* The second problem is the *mul (water) arae (beneath)* image, which is variously interpreted as the bird reflected in the water or as a reference to a village downstream. Either way, the idea would seem to be that the bird (traditionally a Korean hermit's closest companion) has abandoned the narrator, leaving him to utter solitude. The speaker stands with his hand on a moss-flecked plough (which means a useless plough), either because the land is beyond cultivation or because political considerations make cultivation impossible. The speaker's sense of abandonment is complete.

The seventh stanza is also problematical. Deer do not climb poles, and they certainly do not play the Chinese fiddle! A number of interpretations are possible. The narrator may be using metaphor to say that he sees miraculous things from time to time. Or he may be referring to an acrobat on festive occasions climbing a pole, dressed in a deer mask, and playing the fiddle to the delight of the people. A third explanation is that the image denotes sexual congress. The translation accepts the acrobat image at face value. Once again the narrator may be referring to an ideal world: what he hears may be in the mind's ear.

It is not necessary to consider the mountain and sea as totally separate spaces. Both represent an ideal world. The translation takes the view that the poem has a single speaker who does not reach either of these ideal spaces. The speaker is located at the plough, ostracized, utterly alone, but within stone range, which means that his enemies are not far away. His isolation may be as much psychological as physical. None of the detail has to be interpreted realistically; the poem, in fact, will not stand up to such scrutiny. The solitude of the speaker is an imaginative construct, which may have changed considerably as the song passed from generation to generation.

"Ch'ŏngsan pyŏlgok" is a poem of pain and disillusion but not necessarily of despair. The last three stanzas—the delights of the sea, the acrobat's performance on festive occasions, the wine the speaker makes—depict an inner strength that enables the speaker to endure, augmented when necessary with a cup of the good brew. It is an age-old Korean formula for dealing with stress.

> I long, I long,
> for mountains green I long.
> I long to eat wild grapes and berries,
> for mountains green I long.
> Yal-li-yal-li yal-lang-shyŏng yal-la-ri yal-la.
>
> Birds of the air, cry, cry;
> cry when you rise from your nests!
> I have more cares than any bird:

I cry when I rise from my bed.
Yal-li-yal-li yal-lang-shyŏng yal-la-ri yal-la.

Did you see the bird flying?
Did you see it in the water?
My hand is on a moss-flecked plough.
Did you see that bird in the water?
Yal-li-yal-li yal-lang-shyŏng yal-la-ri yal-la.

I pass the day
at this and that,
but how do I pass the night
where no one comes or goes?
Yal-li-yal-li yal-lang-shyŏng yal-la-ri yal-la.

Where was that stone thrown?
At whom was that stone aimed?
With no one to hate and no one to love,
it hurts to be struck, I cry!
Yal-li-yal-li yal-lang-shyŏng yal-la-ri yal-la.

I long, I long,
for the briny sea I long.
To eat fresh kelp, oysters, and crabs
for the briny sea I long.
Yal-li-yal-li yal-lang-shyŏng yal-la-ri yal-la.

I hear wherever I go,
I hear in my favorite places,
I hear the deer on the bamboo pole
playing the Chinese fiddle.
Yal-li-yal-li yal-lang-shyŏng yal-la-ri yal-la.

In a pot-bellied jar wherever I go
I brew a stock of strong raw wine.
The gourd flower yeast makes a potent drink;
what if I toss it all right down?
Yal-li-yal-li yal-lang-shyŏng yal-la-ri yal-la.

SSANGHWA CHŎM (THE *MANDU* SHOP)

"Ssanghwa chŏm" (author unknown) was composed in the reign of Ch'ungnyŏl (1274–1308) and recorded in Akchang kasa. *A dance-drama troupe, composed of kisaeng, female slaves, and female shamans, was organized in Ch'ungyŏl's time. The troupe performed in a special theatre which had been built for them. Songs like "Ssanghwa chŏm" were probably performed there.*

In Chosŏn times this song was classified as immoral. Traditionally it has been interpreted as a satire on the moral decadence of Koryŏ society. The characters in the poem represent the different strata of society: the Turk is a Mongol invader, the monk represents Buddhist circles, the dragon is presumably the king, and the vintner represents the merchant class. This interpretation, however, is at odds with accounts of the song's popularity in the Koryŏ court. Why would a song that points out the corruption of Koryŏ institutions be popular at court? The social allegory approach also ignores the woman who is the speaker, reducing the human content of the poem accordingly. The very heart of the poem is that the speaker is put under no pressure to accede to the requests for sexual favors. She agrees willingly. The question is: does she experience pleasure or frustration? Interpretations of the last two lines in each stanza differ greatly: the room is explained variously as dirty, luxurious, exotic, sultry, full of confusion, and doom-filled. The interpretation of these two lines determines the poem. Is this a young woman who delights in these sexual encounters?

I'll sleep in your privy quarters, I said;
it was sheer luxury where I lay.

Or is it a woman who seeks satisfaction in sexual encounters but finds only disillusion?

Yes, I'll sleep in your privy quarters, I said;
but doom piled high where I lay.

From everything said by Chosŏn authorities about the dissipation of Koryŏ society, the first interpretation seems more likely. However, the image of a young woman at odds with herself, seeking pleasure but filled with misgivings and frustration, makes for greater emotional complexity and a better poem. The translation follows the latter interpretation.

As I was buying dumplings in the *mandu* shop
the playboy Turk took me by the wrist.
Should word *ta-ri-ro* go beyond the shop,
I'll say you made it up, my little player friend.

Ta-ri-ro-di-ro ta-ri-ro-di-ro ta-ri-ro-di-ro-ri-ro.
Yes, I'll sleep in your privy quarters, I said;
but doom piled high where I lay.

As I was lighting a lantern in Samjang Temple
the head monk took me by the wrist.
Should word *ta-ri-ro* go beyond the temple,
I'll say you made it up, my little novice friend.
Ta-ri-ro-di-ro ta-ri-ro-di-ro ta-ri-ro-di-ro-ri-ro.
Yes, I'll sleep in your privy quarters, I said;
but doom piled high where I lay.

As I was drawing water at the village well
the dragon within took me by the wrist.
Should word *ta-ri-ro* go beyond the well,
I'll say you made it up, my little bucket friend.
Ta-ri-ro-di-ro ta-ri-ro-di-ro ta-ri-ro-di-ro-ri-ro.
Yes, I'll sleep in your privy quarters, I said;
but doom piled high where I lay.

As I was buying wine in the vintner's house,
the master of the house took me by the wrist.
Should word *ta-ri-ro* go beyond this house,
I'll say you made it up, my little dipper friend.
Ta-ri-ro-di-ro ta-ri-ro-di-ro ta-ri-ro-di-ro-ri-ro.
Yes, I'll sleep in your privy quarters, I said;
but doom piled high where I lay.

CHŎNGSŎK KA (CHŎNGSŎK'S SONG)

"Chŏngsŏk ka" (author and date unknown) is recorded in Akchang kasa *but is not mentioned in* Koryŏ sa. *Hence it cannot be claimed beyond doubt that it is a Koryŏ song. Traditionally, however, it has been treated as such because of similarities to other Koryŏ songs in theme, mode, and sentiment. The speaker showers her affections on a man named Chŏngsŏk, which literally means gong-stone, a musical instrument. This is a song of undying love rather than a lament for abandonment or unrequited love, which is more common in Korean poetry.*

"Chŏngsŏk ka" consists of six stanzas. An introductory stanza announces that the speaker's love is present; the times are good. The four stanzas with refrains that form the

core of the poem are built on a series of paradoxical statements: chestnut trees flourishing in sand, a carved lotus that blooms, a coat of mail stitched with iron thread, and an iron cow that eats iron grass. As in the case of "Tongdong," nothing remotely like this exists elsewhere in Korean classical poetry. For sheer extravagance of imagination, it is unequaled. The last stanza without a refrain, however, is a bit of a misfit. Identical to the second stanza of "Sǒgyǒng pyǒlgok," it appears to have been added in the process of passing the song down through the generations. The opening stanza may also be an addition, as an introduction to the body of the poem. The gong-stone image has no other connection with the poem.

My gong-stone is here,
my gong-stone is here.
Peaceful times under King Sǒn, a time to play.

Upon a cliff of fine crunchy sand,
upon a cliff of fine crunchy sand,
five bowls of roasted chestnuts I'll plant.
The night they germinate and sprout,
the night they germinate and sprout,
I'll leave my fine, upstanding love.

I'll carve a lotus from a lump of jade,
I'll carve a lotus from a lump of jade,
I'll have it set down roots in rock.
When the lotus blooms three hundred stalks,
when the lotus blooms three hundred stalks,
I'll leave my fine, upstanding love.

I'll make a suit of mail,
I'll make a suit of mail,
I'll stitch the folds with iron thread.
When the suit is worn threadbare,
when the suit is worn threadbare,
I'll leave my fine, upstanding love.

I'll make a cow of iron,
I'll make a cow of iron,
I'll put it on an iron-treed mountain.
When the cow eats iron grass,

when the cow eats iron grass,
I'll leave my fine, upstanding love.

Pearls fall upon the rock,
pearls fall upon the rock,
will the string, the pearl-string snap?
Left alone for a thousand years,
left alone for a thousand years,
will my trust, my love-trust snap?

MANJŎN CH'UN (SPRING PERVADES THE PAVILION)

"Manjŏn ch'un" (author and date unknown) is recorded in Akchang kasa *but not in* Koryŏ sa *or any other historical document. Traditionally it has been treated as a lubricious song, the sentiments of an entertainment woman toward her lover. All the commentators are agreed on the exquisite quality of the opening stanza. Some, however, say that the poem as a whole is very disjointed, perhaps even an amalgam of several poems. The second stanza in particular is full of cliché-ridden Chinese images common in the poetry of the time. They believe that the point of view changes toward the end of the poem, with the man taking over the narration.*

A good case can be made that "Manjŏn ch'un," far from being disjointed and fragmented, is a superb poem with a single narrator and an integrated point of view. The first stanza presents the exquisiteness of sexual love in paradoxically icy terms. The narrator wishes that this night would last forever: love frozen into eternity. The second stanza shows the narrator at home, alone and lonely. Again paradox is at the heart of the imagery: the narrator does not share the spring joy of the blossoms. Her love is not the ephemeral, flirting love associated with peach blossoms. This night cannot end soon enough for the narrator. The cliché-ridden Chinese imagery adds to her discomfort and impatience. In the third stanza the narrator announces that even she is shocked by the profound nature of her love. Such love, she thought, was for others. Some commentators put a different slant on this stanza: she means a love that would last beyond death. This love, however, has been betrayed already; anger and resentment fill her heart.

The fourth stanza has been the center of much discussion. The commentators agree that the duck is the male and the water is the female; the marsh is the narrator and the shallows a rival. They disagree, however, on whether the duck represents the flirtatious original lover or a new candidate for the narrator's affections. A new candidate is rejected by the narrator and sent back to the shallows. That interpretation paves the way for approaching the final stanza as a depiction of ideal love couched in the words of the male but in reality expressing the woman narrator's point of view. This is a dream world, for already the woman has been betrayed. She is finished with her original lover; she has sent the flirtatious second man back to the shallows; and she finishes the poem with a prayer for an ideal lover and a lifetime of fidelity. South Mountain is a house in a prime, sunny location; Jade Mountain is a metaphor for the woman; and Brocade Mountain is their cover in their lovemaking.

Traditionally, the sentiments expressed in this song have been seen as those of a professional entertainer. The idea presumably is that nice Korean women did not entertain such thoughts. This does a disservice to the poem. Not only is this interpretation a denial of sexuality in traditional Korean culture, but it reduces the emotional range of the poem. If the narrator is an entertainment woman, then the last line declares that she is going to change her profession! One section of the poem seems to vindicate the entertainment woman approach, however: the narrator never dreamed that she would know a love like this; she thought such love was for others. It would seem best to leave such questions open. It is sufficient for the reader to be aware of the possibilities.

The bed I make is bamboo leaves: I spread them on the ice.
Though my love and I should freeze unto death,
slowly, slowly, pass this night
in love's enduring gentleness.

I toss and turn in my lonely bed;
I cannot get to sleep.
I open the east window: peach blossoms are in bloom.
Care free, the blossoms scoff at the spring breeze:
   at the spring breeze they scoff.

My spirit one with that of my love!
I thought this was for others.
My spirit one with that of my love!
I thought this was for others.
Who was the transgressor? Who?

"Duck, duck,
my lovely duck,
do you forego the shallows and come to the marsh to sleep?"
"If the marsh freezes, the shallows will suffice,
   the shallows will suffice."

I spread my bed on South Mountain,
pillow my head on Jade Mountain.
Beneath my Brocade Mountain quilt I lie
with a musk sweet girl in my arms.
I spread my bed on South Mountain,
pillow my head on Jade Mountain.
Beneath my Brocade Mountain quilt I lie
with a musk sweet girl in my arms,
breast pressed to fragrant breast,
breast to breast.
Ah, ah, love, let us be true to each other forever.

ISANG KOK (TREADING THE FROST)

"Isang kok" (author and date unknown) is another song strongly reminiscent of the older hyangga. *It is recorded in* Akchang kasa *but not mentioned in* Koryŏ sa. *Thus it cannot be maintained with certainty that it is a Koryŏ song, but traditionally it has been treated as such because of similarities with other Koryŏ songs. One interpretation sees the speaker as a young widow, tempted to take a lover but constrained by thoughts of loyalty to her dead husband; the other sees the speaker as embroiled in an illicit love affair, wondering whether she should follow her heart despite the consequences.*

Some problems arise in interpreting the text. Scholars traditionally treated the third line in Korean (not translated) as nonsense syllables to accompany the music, but recent interpretations suggest a semantic meaning, something like "crouched down tearfully, furtively." Commentators also dispute the subject of line four in the translation. Some contend that the context demands the first-person pronoun, which would mean that the woman narrator is the one on the road, not the lover: "I will not chance to sleep on so dire a road." Without accepting this interpretation, it is difficult to integrate the new approach to the original line three into the text. The translation follows the older interpretation, which sees the line as nonsense syllables to accompany the music; the line is omitted, because it hinders the flow of the song. The phrase yŏlmyŏng kil is interpreted variously as a "dire road" or a "frightening road" or as a reference to the other world.

The poem opens in a powerful vein with rain, snow, wind, and the superb image of frost like a forest of trees—images that drive home the distress of the woman narrator. The narrator thinks of the new man in her life and concludes that he will not come on a night like this. Her moral dilemma places her at hell's door. Each succeeding clap of thunder emphasizes the danger. Should she forsake her old love to walk the rough mountain of new love, with all the social censure that implies? Or should she remember her promise to be true to one man? She concludes that she must keep her promise of fidelity. The translation supports either of these traditional explanations: the widow's dilemma or a woman considering an illicit love affair.

It rained and faired, then the snow flew thick,
and the frost along the narrow winding track was like a forest of trees.
I think of the one who steals my sleep:
no chance he'll dare this road to sleep with me.
With every thunder crash, I stand on hell's doorstep,
a body bound for death.
With every thunder crash, I stand on hell's doorstep,
a body bound for death.
Shall I abjure one love, walk another mountain?
Did we pledge variety,
a little this and a little that?
No, indeed, love. We pledged to go together.

SAMO KOK (SONG TO A MOTHER)

This poem (author and date unknown) is recorded in Akchang kasa. *The central metaphors—hoe and sickle—point to farm origins. Commentators traditionally praise this song as a superb delineation of a mother's love. They talk about the fine use of metaphor and comparison. Apart from the rather obvious statement that the hoe is blunt and the sickle is sharp, however, they do not show how the images actually work in the poem. How do the hoe and sickle mirror a father's and a mother's love? The hoe is a scuffling tool; the sickle is a cutting tool. Is this a poem of praise for a mother's love, of resentment at a father's lack of love, or both? Perhaps it just states the obvious: that a mother's instinctual love is of a higher order than the love of a father.*

A hoe is an edged tool,
but it doesn't cut like a sickle.
A father is a parent,
wi-tŏng-do-tung-schŏng,
but no one loves like a mother.
Believe me, love,
no one loves like a mother.

KASHIRI (MUST YOU GO?)

"Kashiri" (author and date unknown) is another of the songs recorded in Akchang kasa, *which has been treated traditionally as a Koryŏ song based on similarity in content,*

theme, and feeling rather than on any documentary evidence. The knees of the Korean commentators go weak at the mention of "Kashiri." A flood of superlatives follows: exquisite diction, perfection of simplicity, essence of Korean lyricism, blueprint of the Korean heart. It is indeed a lovely folk song, a Korean "Danny Boy." Judged as a love poem, however, it is only a pale shadow of "Sŏgyŏng pyŏlgok" or "Tongdong." The speaker begins by complaining about her lover leaving: "must you?" and "how can you?" She could stop her lover from going, but this would lead to so much resentment that he would never return. In her wisdom, she sends him off with a tearful smile and urges him to come back as soon as he can.

> Must you go, must you go,
> must you leave me so?
> Ah, *chung-jul-ga*, the times are good now.
>
> How can you leave
> with a trite "Fare thee well"?
> Ah, *chung-jul-ga*, the times are good now.
>
> I should stop you, I know,
> but you'd resent it so, you'd never return.
> Ah, *chung-jul-ga*, the times are good now.
>
> So go, my brooding love,
> go, but come right home.
> Ah, *chung-jul-ga*, the times are good now.

HALLIM PYŎLGOK (SONG OF THE SCHOLARS)

This poem is recorded in Akchang kasa. *It belongs to a new poetic genre called* kyŏnggich'e ka. *This name comes from the* kyŏng *character (sight, view) in the fifth line. Only three kyŏnggich'e ka from Koryŏ are extant: "Hallim pyŏlgok," "Kwandong pyŏlgok," and "Chukkye pyŏlgok." "Kwandong pyŏlgok" and "Chukkye pyŏlgok" were composed by An Chuk (1282–1348) and are in a mixture of hyangch'al and Chinese. "Hallim pyŏlgok," which is in Korean and Chinese, is thought to have been composed by Confucian scholars early in the reign of King Kojong of Koryŏ. The Hallim were scholars who turned their backs on the political scene to devote themselves to scholarly pursuits in the tranquillity of nature. Pyŏlgok means special song. Whereas Korean poetry traditionally focuses on emotional states, the commentators note that the kyŏnggich'e ka focuses on external objects, showing the new interest of the literati in objective reality. It is unlikely, however, that a Western reader will see "Hallim pyŏlgok" as a manifesto of realism!*

"Hallim pyŏlgok" is a listing of leisurely pursuits and the pleasures of the scholarly life: literature, poetry, calligraphy, music, wine, trees, beautiful places, and beautiful women. The poem names the greatest poets in the land and suggests that a gathering of these worthies in the Examination Hall would be a wonderful sight. It lists the great poets of classical China and the great classical texts and names Korea's greatest talents in calligraphy and music. The poem catalogs the finest wines, the loveliest trees, and the most beautiful places in the land. It ends with a description of the delights of being on a swing with a lovely lady—from the sublime to the titivating!

To appreciate "Hallim pyŏlgok" the reader must imagine it in performance: king and nobles gathered for a banquet, tables laden with food, wine flowing in rivers. The musicians strike the opening chord; the kisaeng rise, swaying to the dance; the nobles raise their goblets in the toast. Against this background, a pedestrian poem becomes a colorful pageant of song, dance, and feasting. This is a song of Korean hŭng (the buzz of excitement associated with the apprehension of beauty)! It did not seem necessary to dot the text with notes identifying the various historical characters. The spelling indicates which names are Korean and which are Chinese; and the expertise of each person is apparent from the context. Most of the musicians are not recorded in any other document; some are known simply as kisaeng. The stanza on the mountains of the Immortals describes an ideal world where a beautiful lady lives in a red pavilion. The poem suggests connections between this lady and a poem by Bai Juyi (772–846, Middle Tang), but the commentators believe that the mountains are in Korea not in China. The narrator looks at the banquet unfolding before him and is carried in spirit to an ideal world of the Immortals. Correspondences with actual places and people are not important. The final stanza describes ideal beauty in the company of a lovely lady. Again the narrator's vision is prompted by the banquet scene.

Yu Wŏnsun for diction; Yi Illo for poetry; Yi Kongro for four- and
　　six-character parallel lines;
Yi Kyubo and Chin Hwa for ex tempore rhyming couplets;
Yu Ch'unggi for criticism; Min Kwanggyun for explication;
　　Kim Yanggyŏng for rhyme.
Ah ah, the Examination Hall, what a wonderful sight!
Students of Master Kŭm Ŭi, in lines like bamboo shoots!
Students of Master Kŭm Ŭi, in lines like bamboo shoots!
Ah ah, how many, myself included?

For prose style, the *History of Tang*, the *History of Han*; Zhuang Zi,
　　Lao Zi; Han Yu and Liu Zongyuan.
For poetry, Li Bai, Du Fu, *Collection of the Orchid Terrace*, Bai Juyi,

The Book of Songs and The Book of Documents, The Book of Changes,
   The Spring and Autumn Annals, The Great Book of Ceremonies and
   The Small Book of Ceremonies.
Ah, ah, recited with all the footnotes, what a wonderful sight!
The four hundred scrolls of the Broad Record of the Taiping Era,
the four hundred scrolls of the Broad Record of the Taiping Era,
ah ah, reading them through, what a wonderful sight!

Yan Chenqing for calligraphy; flying, cursive, and script style;
seal script large, seal script small, tadpole script.
Brushes made from goat or rat whiskers, held at the angle.
Ah ah, the character strokes, what a wonderful sight!
Master O and Master Yu,
Master O and Master Yu,
ah ah, brushes flying down the page. What a wonderful sight!

Wine—Yellow-Gold, Pine-Nut, Pine-Leaf, Sweet Wine,
Bamboo-Leaf, Pear-Flower, Angelica—
brimming in pearl and amber cups.
And when the goblets are proffered in the toast, ah ah, what a
   wonderful sight!
Liu Ling and Tao Yuanming, the two old Immortals,
Liu Ling and Tao Yuanming, the two old Immortals,
ah ah, drunk as coots, what a wonderful sight!

Peony tree—crimson, white, and purple;
Peony flower—crimson, white, and purple;
pomegranate-ume, red and yellow rose, camellia,
ah ah, all in a riot of blossom, what a wonderful sight!
Folded bamboo and peach, two noble friends,
folded bamboo and peach, two noble friends,
ah ah, they look each other in the face. What a wonderful sight!

Ah Yang on the kŏmun'go, Mun T'ak on the flute, Chong Mu on the
   fiddle;
Taeŏhyang and Okkihyang on twin kayagŭm;
Kim Sŏn on pip'a lute, Chong Chi on two-string fiddle, Sŏl Wŏn
   on drum.

Ah ah, music through the night, what a wonderful sight!
Ilchihong on the transverse flute,
Ilchihong on the transverse flute;
Ah ah, sweet music lulls me to sleep.

Pongnae Mountain, Pangjang Mountain, Yŏngju, the three mountains
    of the Immortals
where the lovely fairy lady of the Red Pavilion dwells,
bead curtain half raised in the room with embroidered silk hangings.
Ah, ah, looking out across the lake: what a wonderful sight!
Behind the pavilion on the green-willow-bamboo knoll,
ah ah, how lovely to hear the call of oriole and parakeet!

The swing is slung on a purple rope
between the walnut and the honey locust.
Pull, push, my lad.
Ah ah, let no one follow my path.
Two lovely hands, lovely as silk,
fashioned as it were from carved jade.
I take your lovely hands in mine.
Ah ah, swinging together, a vision of silk fashioned from carved jade,
what a wonderful sight!

YUGU KOK (SONG OF THE CUCKOO)

This poem (author and date unknown) is recorded in Shiyong hyangakpo. *"Yugu kok" had been lost for centuries, except for a reference in* Koryŏ sa *to "Pŏlgokcho ka" by the Koryŏ king Yejong (1079–1122), presumably the same poem with a different title. It surfaced belatedly in 1954 with the introduction of* Shiyong hyangakpo *to the academic world. This poem exemplifies the best in Koryŏ songs: simple, artless, it goes straight to the marrow. Even with the conventional explanation that the cuckoo is the voice of the people while the dove represents the voice of officialdom, the poem rings out. Cuckoo song and pigeon coo are in lovely contrast; the two birds, with their opposing characters, act out a little drama full of human implications.*

The pigeon,
the pigeon
has a doleful coo;

the cuckoo,
the cuckoo
is the bird
I woo.

SANGJŎ KA (SONG OF THE MILL)

"Sangjŏ ka" (author and date unknown) was discovered in Shiyong hyangakpo *in 1954. It is presumed to be an old folk song, dating perhaps from pre-Koryŏ times, a work song for grinding grain. In literary terms it does not offer much except a picture of the simple lifestyle of past times and a testament to the Confucian mode of family life.*

Tŏlk-kŏ-dong the mill grinds.
I'll cook a pot of yellow coarse rice
and offer it to my dad and mum.
If there's any left I'll eat it myself.
Hi-ya-hae hi-ya-hae.

NARYE KA (SONG OF EXORCISM)

This poem (author and date unknown) is recorded in Shiyong hyangakpo. *Narye was a ritual to expel evil spirits; it was performed on the last day of the year both in the court and in the houses of the people. Chinese in its origins, the ritual was popular in the Koryŏ court. It was often linked in performance to "Ch'ŏyong ka," a dramatic dance ritual that survived into Chosŏn.* Kut *is a shaman ritual.*

On the day of the exorcism in Lord Nayŏng's hall,
the clowns dress in striped cloth of gold.
When there's a performance of the mountain *kut*,
even the demons are arrayed in striped cloth of gold.
Ri-ra-ri-ro na-ri-ra ri-ra-ri.

TAEWANG PAN (RITUAL OFFERING TO THE GREAT KING)

This poem (author and date unknown) is recorded in Shiyong hyangakpo.

The eight protector gods,
the eight protector gods

amuse themselves and rest by turns;
amorous pursuits spectacular!
My Lord is at play:
women numerous as the black peonies
that fill the capital.
Ti-ro-rong-ta-ri ta-ri-ro-ti-ro-ri.

Koryŏ *Hanshi* and *Shijo*

Classical literature contains no references to a genre called *shijo*; traditionally the term refers to a musical mode. *Kasa* (literally, "music words") was the term used to describe all vernacular songs. The songs we call *shijo* today are a subdivision of *kasa*; they were sung originally to the *kagok-ch'ang*, a complex music accompaniment with five sung *chang* (sections) and two musical interludes. Less than twenty songs with claims to go back to Koryŏ are recorded in the great *shijo* anthologies, which date from the eighteenth century. Ch'oe Tong'wŏn says that only eight Koryŏ poets have credible credentials: U T'ak, Yi Cho'nyŏn, Ch'oe Yŏng, Sŏng Yŏwan, Chŏng Mongju, Yi Chono, Yi Saek, and T'aejong.[5] Kwŏn Tuhwan doubts the ascription of "Hayŏ ka" and "Tanshim ka."[6]

The term *shijo* began to be used in reference to a literary text in the 1920s, when the nationalist leadership of the period saw the possibilities of the form as a vehicle to raise national consciousness. The essential criteria for *shijo* were soon firmly established: they were three-*chang* (section) poems with fourteen to sixteen syllables in each *chang*, distributed in four distinct *ŭmbo* or breath-groups; the total number of syllables was not more than forty-five.

This critical framework held sway for twenty years. By the 1950s, however, scholars were questioning the enormous number of exceptions to the ideal count as postulated in the various syllable count systems. Several new theories of the rhythmic structure of *shijo* were introduced. The new theories ran the gamut of prosodic possibility, from metrical theories with accented and unaccented syllables to theories of tone (pitch) and quantity (*changdan*: long, short). None of these theories provided real satisfaction. Ultimately, all that could be said with certainty was that the *ŭmbo* or breath-group is the fundamental unit of *shijo* and that the rhythm of all Korean writing, both prose and poetry, is 3/4.

5. Ch'oe Tong'wŏn, *Koshijo non'go*, p. 17.
6. Kwŏn Tuhwan, "Shijoǔi palsaenggwa kiwŏn," in Kungmun hakhoe, ed., *Koshijo yŏn'gu*, p. 10.

Scholars until very recently treated the *shijo* almost exclusively as literary texts, paying only lip service to the music. The genre was seen variously as developing from Shilla *hyangga*, from the Koryŏ *tan'ga*, from ancient shamanistic chants, from the process of translating Chinese poems into Korean, or from Buddhist songs in China. In recent years, however, scholars have begun to look for the sources of *shijo* in musical tradition. All agree that originally the music was integral to the form. Despite all the prosodic analysis of the last fifty years, however, the three-*chang* division of the *shijo* text, introduced by Ch'oe Namsŏn in the 1920s, is still a dominant concept, so imbedded in the popular consciousness as to be virtually unassailable. Accordingly, the *shijo* translations in this volume employ the three-*chang* structure, but they do so in combination with a five-line English format that corresponds broadly to the five-part song structure of the *kagok-ch'ang* to which the songs were originally sung.

The five-line format is primarily a visual device. *Shijo* were traditionally translated into English in a six-line and (less commonly) a three-line format. I developed the five-line format not just because it was warranted by the history of the *shijo*, but also because it opens up huge possibilities in English. The translations attempt to get something of the feel of the *kagok* back into the literary text, to approximate in English the Korean sense of poetic excitement (*hŭng*) that is at the heart of the *shijo* experience. The five-line format brings the uniqueness of the *shijo* home to the reader through the appearance of the songs on the page. The shape of the *shijo* and the *shijo's* prosy-recitative quality come across in a way not hitherto possible: the unusual five-line format, the varying line lengths (especially the longer third and fifth lines), and the three-syllable fourth line all contribute to presenting in English something uniquely Korean and totally new in Western poetry experience. (For a full treatment of the *shijo* form, see Cho Kyuik, *Kagokch'angsaŭi kungmunhakchŏk ponjil* [The Essence of the *Kagok-ch'ang* Song Lyric in the Korean Literature Tradition], and Kevin O'Rourke, *The Book of Korean Shijo*).

CH'OE CH'UNG, 984–1068

Ch'oe Ch'ung, a Confucian scholar during the reign of the Koryŏ king Munjong, was known as the Confucius of the East Sea.

Pungmang Mountain in China was synonymous with the graveyard, death, or Hades.

SHIJO 895

The searing sun sets on West Mountain;
the Yellow River flows into the East Sea.
Do the heroes of yesterday and today go in death to Pungmang
    Mountain?
So be it:
all things wax and wane; is there any point in regret?

SHIJO 1735
Fu Xi was a king in old China who lived in a time of great peace.

All my life I regret
that I wasn't born in the time of Fu Xi.
The people may have worn grass clothes and eaten berries,
but they retained
the warmth of their dispositions: this I shall envy always.

HYŎNJONG, 992–1031

Hyŏnjong was Koryŏ's eighth monarch. At the age of twelve he shaved his head and be-came a monk. He ascended the throne in 1006.

BABY SERPENT (*hanshi*)

The serpent is presumably a reference to the Korean mythical imugi, *a serpent that changes into a dragon. Hyŏnjong has apparently given up all thought of the throne and suddenly realizes the possibilities of becoming king.*

Baby serpent, entwined around the peony railing,
body dappled with crimson silk,
don't say you'll spend your life in the flower forest;
in the space of a morning you could easily become a dragon.

PAK ILLYANG, ?–1096

Pak Illyang was an official in the Koryŏ court. His reputation for poetry composition extended to far-off Song China, which he visited as an emissary of the Koryŏ court.

SENT TO SONG CHINA BY WAY OF KUSAN-SA
(TORTOISE MOUNTAIN TEMPLE) IN SIZHOU (*hanshi*)
Paduk is a popular board game.

The mountain is rough rock layers and strange shaped stones;
a lotus pond on top, water all around.
The shadow of the pagoda, upside down, shimmers in the water.
Windbells shake the moon till it falls through the clouds.
The guest at the gate rowed urgently through rough waves.
Under the bamboo stalks monks play *paduk* leisurely through the day.
I am the king's messenger; parting is inevitable.
I leave behind a poem and a promise to return.

SONG OF NIGHT ON A BOAT (*hanshi*)
This poem was written when the poet, an emissary to Song, spent a night on lovely Dongting Lake in China.

The ancient land of Koryŏ is far away;
autumn breezes blow; confusion fills the wayfarer's heart.
A night's dreams on a lonely boat
spread in waves across the moonlit waters of Dongting Lake.

KIM PUSHIK, 1075–1151

Kim Pushik was a scholar-official and military commander in Koryŏ. He edited Samguk sagi (Records of the Three Kingdoms), a fifty-volume compendium of all things Korean. Patterned after the dynastic histories of China, it expresses a Confucian point of view.

Kim Pushik put down the Myoch'ŏng Insurrection in Pyŏngyang in 1135 and was a prominent figure in the subsequent Confucian regime.

SWEET DEW TEMPLE: IN REPLY TO A RHYME OF HYEWŎN (*hanshi*)
Kamno-sa (Sweet Dew Temple) was in Kaesŏng in Kyŏnggi Province.

This is no place for a worldling guest;
thought grows lucid when you get to the top.
The mountain is in autumn mode; all the better;
the color of the river is even clearer at night.
A white heron disappears in solitary flight;
a solitary sailboat glides lightly on the water.
Shame on me: for half a lifetime I've sought
fame and honor in a constricted world.

CHŎNG CHISANG, ?—1135

Chŏng Chisang was born in P'yŏngyang. An official in the Koryŏ court, he was skilled in poetry, painting, calligraphy, and divination. He was also deeply interested in Buddhist lore and in the teachings of Lao Zi and Zhuang Zi. Accusations of involvement in the Myoch'ŏng Insurrection in P'yŏngyang in 1135, which his rival Kim Pushik quelled, cost him his life.

SEEING OFF A FRIEND (*hanshi*)
Namp'o is a town near P'yŏngyang, North Korea.

How green the grass on the long bank now that the rain has cleared!
I send my love to Namp'o; a sad song lingers on my lips.
When will the waters of the Taedong dry,
augmented year after year by the tears of those who have parted?

SEND-OFF (*hanshi*)
A single leaf falls in the garden;
beneath my bed a hundred insects cry.
So sudden—impossible to stop;
So self-possessed—where is he going?
My fractured heart runs to the mountain end.
I dream a lonesome dream under the bright moon.
Do not disavow our pledge to meet again
when the spring wave is blue at Namp'o.

TINY ROOM IN FLOWER SAGE TEMPLE (*hanshi*)
Kaesŏng-sa is in Hwanghae Province, North Korea.

Nine turns in a hundred paces, I climb the high mountain.
The house hangs in the air—it only has a few rooms.
The sacred spring is clear; cool water flows.
Old dark walls are spotted as if with green moss.
A stone-head pine ages under a sliver moon.
Clouds drape a thousand mountain peaks at the rim of the sky.
The dust of human affairs cannot reach this far;
leisure is the hermit's joy through the years!

SUMMER CLOUDS (*hanshi*)
Sunny day: in the heart of the sky
floating clouds form peaks.
A monk at the sight wonders if there's a temple there.
A crane looking on regrets the absence of pine.
A flash of lightning is the woodsman's axe;
a peal of thunder is the bell of the hidden temple.
Who said mountains don't move?
In the wind that rises with the fading light they fly!

CHŎNG SŬMMYŎNG, ?—1151

Chŏng Sŭmmyŏng, an ancestor of the great Chŏng Mongju, was an official in Koryŏ. The vitality, color, and sensuality of this poem show the heart of Koryŏ poetry.

CHINA PINKS (*hanshi*)
The world loves the red peony;
the garden is full of them.
Who knows that fine flowers
cluster in wild fields?
Colors flicker in the moonlit lotus pond;
fragrance is borne by the wind in the trees.
Few guests grace this barren place;
such sexy loveliness is an old farmer's privilege.

KO CHOGI, ?—1157

Ko Chogi, a native of Cheju Island, was a Koryŏ scholar-official.

RAINY NIGHT IN A MOUNTAIN VILLA (*hanshi*)
Last night it rained on Pine Pavilion;
the tinkling stream was my pillow.
I look at the garden trees in the dawn;
sleeping birds have not flown the roost.

ANSŎNG POSTHOUSE (*hanshi*)
Ansŏng in Kyŏnggi Province was noted for its brassware. Hence the expression "Ansŏng match'um" (literally, "ordered in Ansŏng") to denote something of superior quality.

Mountain rain deters travelers;
day draws to a close in the posthouse inn.
Spring rain is empty of good and bad;
sheer physicality scratches itself everywhere.
Willow eyes already are blissfully open;
Flower lips assay gentle smiles.
Why hasn't my hair
changed from last year's silver?

KIM KŬKKI, 1148?–1209

Kim Kŭkki passed the civil service examination, but he was a poet by sensibility and had little time for power. Travel and country life had much greater appeal than the stress of public life. Eventually he was appointed to the staff of the Royal Academy and he died soon after. He is a poet of considerable power. His scenes of rural life are unequaled in Koryŏ. Nature speaks through frogs and magpies. The two drunk old men riding off, back to front on horseback, show real human warmth.

FARMHOUSES (*hanshi*)
There are two or three houses where the blue mountain ends
and a winding track that circles the hill.
Frogs croak in a dried-up hole—it's going to rain.
Magpies squawk in the high trees—it's going to blow.
The willow-lined lane is buried gently in grass.
No one at home; fallen petals cover the brushwood gate.
It's a real joy to be at ease beyond the dusty world.
Those who sedulously seek the dazzle seem foolish in comparison.

GROWING OLD (*hanshi*)
Composition provides mutual joy as we age.
I may wield a sword on the frontier, but five carts of books are my store.
I finish official business, forget about front-line duties,
lie down and read in a bright spot under the paper window.

Open books fill the room: they're scattered dizzily all around.
I awaken, get up; already the sun is low on the eaves to the west.
Where did that sparrow make its nest?
It flies down to the stone steps to peck at grains of fallen rice.

KOWŎN POSTHOUSE (*hanshi*)

This fleeting life is a hundred years; and already I'm fifty.
Life's road is rough, the ferries are few.
It's three years since I left Seoul; what have I achieved?
After a thousand miles of road, this body is all I bring home.
Birds in the forest are in sympathy; they cry when they see a wayfarer.
Flowers in the fields say nothing, but they hold me with their smiles.
Everywhere I go I'm asked for a poem; I'm beset by a devil within.
He may not be my ruin, but the travail he brings is a bitter thing.

TWO OLD MEN FROM THE VILLAGE BRING WINE
TO THE CHARCOAL HOUSE (*hanshi*)

Deeper and deeper they venture down the weed-clogged track,
they tie their horses to a withered willow branch.
Where are they from, these two white-haired old men
plodding shoulder to shoulder?
I serve dried fish on a tray of mountain eats;
they have *makkŏlli* in their country picnic basket.
In the village I'm the subject of idle scorn and banter;
a crazy man, hair a wet tangle.
Here ceremony gradually becomes redundant;
warm affection suffices.
They return to the village by the way they came,
back to front on their horses;
the village children will surely applaud.

YI ILLO, 1152–1220

Yi Illo was a scholar and poet and a representative figure in Koryŏ's cultural life, noted for his skill in poetry and calligraphy and for his love of wine. He held several high-ranking offices in the Koryŏ court.

MOUNTAIN HUT (*hanshi*)

Spring has gone but flowers still bloom.
The sky is bright, but the valley is in shade.
The scops owl cries in the daylight hours.
Now I know how secluded my hut is.

NIGHT RAIN ON THE XIAOXIANG (*hanshi*)
The Xiao and the Xiang are tributaries of the Yangtze.

A stretch of blue water divides autumn shores;
the wind blows a fine rain on my homing boat.
Night comes; I tie up in riverside bamboo.
Each shivering leaf voices all my cares.

READING TAO YUANMING'S LIFE (*hanshi*)
Chinese poet, official, wine-bibber, devotee of the simple life in nature, Tao Yuanming
(365–427) was much admired by Korean poets.

"What's so great about drinking?"
Words with the taste of truth!
Funny how Tao Yuanming enjoyed his wine
even though he hadn't any money!
I'm a simple man by nature, no way greedy,
not tied to material things,
never drunk, never sober.
I find myself very close to nature's core.

YI KYUBO, 1168–1241

Yi Kyubo lived during a very turbulent period of Korean history: Koryŏ was threatened
to the north by barbarian tribes and from within by factionalism in the bureaucracy. Not
belonging to one of the old distinguished Confucian families, he had to rely on his own abil-
ities to nurture his career as one of the new elite that emerged after the military coup of
1170. He failed the civil service examination three times before eventually passing in 1189.
His failures were not due to any lack of ability—he was a child prodigy—but rather due to
a propensity to drink too much wine and to do very little formal study. Yi Kyubo entered
the civil service late and had a long career, which was punctuated by demotion, dismissal,
and exile. He experienced more than his share of bitterness and frustration. A chance meet-
ing with General Ch'oe Ch'unghŏn, who was the powerhouse in the government after the
successful revolt in 1196, led to recognition of his talents and preferment. General Ch'oe's
son, Ch'oe I, was a lifelong mentor.

Yi Kyubo is one of Korea's greatest poets. His poems are vibrantly alive. Solidly
grounded in the feelings and concerns of everyday life, they offer brief but brilliant illumi-
nations of the heart. In poetry Yi Kyubo was very much his own man, taking from the Chi-
nese tradition what he thought suited the Korean situation. Thus he was constrained by

neither the Tang nor the Song poetry tradition. He valued content above form, ki *(energy) above decoration. He wrote Old Style as well as Modern Style. Several thousand of his* han-shi *are extant; they are collected in* Tongguk Yi Sangguk chip *(Collected Works of Minister Yi from the Eastern Kingdom).*

ON THE ROAD: HEARING THE SOUNDS OF
PADUK STONES IN A PAVILION (*hanshi*)
Paduk *is a popular board game with black and white counters.*

Behind the bamboo curtain shadows are indistinct;
paduk stones rattle across the board like hail after rain has cleared.
Skill, great or little, is irrelevant here;
the pleasure is in the clinking of the stones.

SONG OF THE PAULOWNIA (*hanshi*)
Shade once a broad thick curtain
now swirling leaves scatter like beads.
Planted originally for the noble phoenix,
a ragged motley nests here now.

BURNING MY MANUSCRIPTS (*hanshi*)
In my youth I used to write songs.
When the brush moved down the page,
I wrote with unimpeded flow.
My poems, I thought, were as beautiful as jade;
who dared talk about flaws?
Afterward, I studied them again:
there wasn't a fine word in one of them.
To retain them would be to soil my writing box:
unbearable thought, so I burned them in the kitchen fire.
If I look next year at this year's poems,
they will all be the same; I'll scrap them too.
Perhaps that's why Minister Kao of old
first composed when he was fifty.

DRINKING COLD WINE WITH A GUEST ONE WINTER'S DAY:
COMPOSED PLAYFULLY (*hanshi*)
Snow fills the capital; the price of charcoal has soared.

Cold bottle, frozen hands; the fragrant *makkŏlli* is poured.
Don't you know how wine in the belly soon generates its own heat?
I suggest you wait for the rose afterglow to come into your cheeks.

WRITTEN ON THE UPPER STORY OF YOSŎNG POSTHOUSE (*hanshi*)
When the mood comes, I order a carriage; when I feel tired, I rest.
A thousand thanks to heaven and earth for freeing me for such leisure.
I feel sorry for the white-haired official who works the station;
he's cast an entire life between the hooves of a horse.

RESTING AT SIHU INN (*hanshi*)
Excessive thirst is an old complaint.
Muggy summer's day; I set out again on a long journey.
With a pot of tea I try an experiment in taste;
it's like frozen snow going down my throat.
I rest again in the pine pavilion;
already I feel autumn in every bone.
The lad can't understand me at all;
he thinks it weird I delay so long.
My disposition has always been broad and liberal:
when I get to a place, I stay as long as I want;
when I meet an obstruction, immediately I stop;
when I ride a river, I float.
What's the harm in staying here?
What's in it for me if I go there?
There's a lot of space between sky and earth;
my life has tranquillity.

EVENING ON THE MOUNTAIN: SONG TO THE MOON IN THE WELL
I (*hanshi*)
Blue water ripples the well at the corner of the mossy rock.
The new moon is beautifully etched therein.
I scoop out some water, but only a shadow enters my jar.
I fear I'll bring only half the golden mirror home.

EVENING ON THE MOUNTAIN: SONG TO THE MOON IN THE WELL
2 (*hanshi*)
A mountain monk coveted the moon;
he drew water, a whole jar full;
but when he reached his temple, he discovered
that tilting the jar meant spilling the moon.

POETRY: A CHRONIC DISEASE (*hanshi*)
I'm over seventy now,
an official of the first rank;
I know I should give up poetry,
but somehow I can't.
Mornings I sing like a cricket;
evenings I hoot like an owl.
I'm possessed by a devil I can't exorcise;
night and day it follows me stealthily around.
Once possessed I never have a moment free;
a pretty mess it's got me in.
Day after day I shrivel heart and liver
just to write a few poems.
Body fats and fluids depleted,
there's nothing left but skin and grizzle.
Bones protruding, struggling to recite,
I make a very foolish figure.
I have no words to elicit wonder,
nothing to pass on that will last a thousand years.
I clap my hands, guffaw, and when the laughter
bout subsides, I begin to recite again.
My life and death hang on poetry;
not even a physician could cure this disease.

VISIT TO THE HERMITAGE OF MASTER KA, USING A RHYME WRITTEN
ON THE WALL BY SOMEONE LONG DEAD (*hanshi*)
Desolate the monk's room beside the ancient tree;
one lamp, one incense burner in the shrine.
No need to ask the old monk how he spends his days.
A chat when a guest comes; when he goes, a nap.

SUMMER DAY HAPPENING (*hanshi*)

I put on my light summer coat and lie down on the small bamboo mat
    to catch the breeze on the veranda.
The song of the golden oriole interrupts my dream.
Flowers shaded by clustered leaves live on when spring has gone;
sunlight filtering through light clouds shines brightly in the rain.

ONCE AGAIN TO THE RHYME OF "LEASING A STRAW HUT" (*hanshi*)

Better become an old tiller of the soil
than shame myself by buying preferment.
If you live on a government stipend
you're like a monkey in a cage: you eat what you get.
I want to forget the world and fly like a bird.
The deeper you hide jade the more it asserts its beauty;
why should the orchid be sad because it's not plucked?
My singular joy is to have clusters of black-haired children
running around my sleeping bench.

WRITTEN ON THE WALL AFTER ARRIVING
AT DRAGON ROCK TEMPLE (*hanshi*)

Yong'am-sa (Dragon Rock Temple) is in Hwasun, Chŏlla Province.

Here in the flesh at Dragon Rock Temple, I wonder if this is where the
    Immortals live?
With my lips I test Turtle Spring; the water tastes like an ice drink.
A thousand pieces of gold would not buy the flavor of the monk's
    house.
Rain falling on the mountain, I get myself some sleep.

CHINA ROSE (*hanshi*)

I wanted to bloom with spring blossoms, but too soon they dropped
    with the wind.
I wanted to bloom with fall's fragrant crop, but this too became an
    empty dream.
A thorough screening of the flowers around me revealed no suitable
    companion;
so fresh and lone, I kept my red youth for the snow.

VIEW FROM MY STRAW HUT (*hanshi*)
My cute daughter chases a butterfly; the butterfly flutters.
My little son catches a cicada; the cicada buzzes.
I read a bit, doze a bit, try to read what's left;
the words drift gradually to slurred somniloquence.

PRESENTED TO A *KISAENG* AT A DRINKING PARTY
AFTER AN ILLNESS (*hanshi*)
Wine has me dancing and singing for joy;
medicine makes my sick body fly.
Who unfolds the glory of spring again in an old man's eyes?
A *kisaeng* with jade face smiles a gracious smile.

FARMHOUSE: THREE POEMS (*hanshi*)
The village mill echoes through wispy smoke crisscrosses.
There are no walls along the length of the lane; clustered thorny trees
    are demarcators here.
Horses dot the mountain; cattle are scattered through the fields.
Everywhere I see the face of a great age of peace.

The loom importunes in the heavy frost and chill of dawn.
In the darkening smoke of the setting sun, the woodcutter sings as he
    returns.
How could an old countryman know the ninth day of the ninth
    month?
Yet he dips in his mellow wine those yellow chrysanthemums he
    chanced upon.

The leaves of the mountain pear are red; yellow the leaves of the
    mulberry.
Along the road the breeze returns, thick with the fragrance of rice
    stalks.
The sound of water being scooped from the well is echoed in the
    wooden clogs;
through the open brushwood gate, moonlight carpets the frost.

THE SECRETARY GOT A BEAUTIFUL *KISAENG* TO BRING ME PAPER
AND REQUEST A POEM; MY BRUSH FLEW AND I PRESENTED THIS
(*hanshi*)
The heart of the man becomes the heart of a girl;
in the moment of parting, tears fondly sprinkle my collar.
The wayfarer's bag is empty; it holds nothing fine.
I'll give you a poem; it's worth a thousand gold coins.

MAKKŎLLI SONG (*hanshi*)
Makkŏlli *is unrefined rice wine.*

In the old wandering, carefree days
makkŏlli was my regular drink,
and if, on occasion, I got clear wine,
I couldn't resist the glow of a binge.
But when I rose to high station,
there was no reason to have *makkŏlli*.
Now I'm old and retired, my stipend is reduced,
the rice bin is often empty.
Good wine is a commodity that comes and goes,
and *makkŏlli* occasions are starting to grow.
Makkŏlli lies on the stomach; it clogs the digestion;
now I know the evils of cheap wine.
Du Fu claimed, though I didn't understand at the time,
that *makkŏlli* was a receptacle of the sublime.
I understand now:
personality is colored by living standards;
food follows status;
how could likes and dislikes be of consequence?
Thus I tell my wife to be frugal with what goes out,
no matter how much is coming in,
and when she fills the wine-jar, I tell her
not to fill it with water-clear wine.

SELF-DERISION (*hanshi*)
My shoulders are cold, the bones stick up;
my hair is diseased, stubbly and sparse as mugwort.
Who said I was to be the last of the honest men,

that I shouldn't fold and unfold with the times?
When deceit is rampant, there are tigers in the marketplace;
when justice reigns, there are no fish in the water.
Perhaps it's best if I become an old farmer,
go back to the plough and daily carry the hoe.

READING TAO YUANMING'S POEMS (*hanshi*)
Poet-official, wine-bibber, devotee of the simple life in nature, Tao Yuanming (365–427)
from East Jin was much admired by Korean poets.

I love Tao Yuanming;
his poems are limpid and pure.
He always strummed a stringless lyre;
his poems have that same quiet grace.
Sublime rhythm is of its nature soundless;
there's no need to strum the lyre.
Sublime language is of its nature worldless;
it's not necessary to carve and trim.
This is a wisdom that springs from nature,
the longer chewed the better the taste.
Tao Yuanming freed himself from official business:
    he returned to the country,
to wander among pine, bamboo, and chrysanthemum.
When he had no wine, he sought out a friend;
he fell down drunk every day.
On the sleeping bench he stretched his body out;
the breeze blew cool and refreshing.
From the bright ancient world he came,
a scholar noble and true.
I think of the man when I read the poems;
his integrity will be praised for a thousand years.

PRESENTED TO CHŎN IJI ON A VISIT:
WE DRANK TOGETHER AND GOT TERRIBLY DRUNK (*hanshi*)
Chŏn Iji was a good friend of Yi Kyubo. Little is known about him. He was obviously
the retiring type: Yi Kyubo notes in a letter to Ch'oe Cha, whom he held in the highest es-
teem, that Chŏn Iji's writing was of exceptional quality but that no one knew about it.

A close friend came on a visit:
my circumstances, however, were so straitened I couldn't buy wine.
He sat down, leisure written on his face:
I knew we couldn't spend the whole day in talk.
So I pawned the old rags on my back,
exchanging them for a jar of clear brimming wine.
Cup after cup we tilted till the wine joy came on us;
we seemed to gallop like crazy horses loosed from the bridle.
My songs shook the trees in the forest;
his brush made the river reverse its current.
My songs grew coarse as if washing away resentment;
his brush sped with cruel intent as if discharging anger.
Who was wise and who was foolish,
who had gained and who had lost?
The man who gained was not necessarily wise;
the covetous and the mean rise to high station.
The man who lost was not necessarily foolish;
the illustrious in thought and deed live in poverty.
Forget about me—I'm insignificant—but my friend,
a great man, a hero, why has he no official rank?
Rogues rise up while good men stay stuck to the ground.
The crooked seize their opportunity;
the straight are put to rout.
Discussing the affairs of a lifetime with you,
I spat out in wine things that always weighed me down.
By turns I caressed my long-sword, danced, sat and drank again,
a cup, then another and another . . .

THINKING OF MY CHILDREN: FIRST OF TWO POEMS (*hanshi*)
I have a young daughter;
already she knows how to call her dad and mom.
She drags her skirt along and plays at my knees;
she takes the mirror and imitates her mother at makeup.
How many months now since we parted?
Suddenly it's as if she were by my side.
By nature I'm a wanderer;
dejected, I live in this foreign place.

For weeks I've been on a binge;
I've been laid up sick for a month.
I turn my head and look toward the palace in Seoul;
mountains and streams stretch oppressively far.
This morning suddenly I thought of you;
tears flowed down, wetting my skirt.
Boy, hurry and feed the horse;
my desire to go home grows more urgent
with every passing day.

HOW I FELT PAWNING MY COAT: SHOWN TO CH'OE CHONGBŎN
(*hanshi*)
Ch'oe Chongbŏn was appointed a royal secretary in 1228.

Third month, eleventh day;
no reason to light the kitchen fire this morning.
The wife said she'd pawn my fur;
I scolded her at first and stopped her.
Suppose the cold has already gone,
what pawnbroker would take the coat?
Suppose the cold returns,
how am I to survive the winter?
The wife retorted angrily:
how can you be so foolish?
I know it's not the most glorious coat ever,
but the thread was woven by these hands;
I grudge it twice as much as you,
but mouth and belly are more urgent than furs.
A man who doesn't eat twice a day, the ancients say,
is heading for starvation,
and a starving man can drop, morning or evening;
so how can you promise yourself another winter?
I called the servant and sent him at once to sell the fur.
I thought we'd survive for several days on the proceeds,
but what the servant brought back was no equivalent.
Suspicious, I suggested he might have pocketed some for himself.
The servant's face went an angry color.

He quoted the pawnbroker:
already summer encroaches on what's left of spring,
is it reasonable to buy furs at a time like this?
The only reason I'm willing to parry winter early
is that I have a little extra.
If I didn't have that bit to spare,
I wouldn't give you a single bag of grain.
Hearing this, I was ashamed, ashamed;
tears flowed down and wet my chin.
Fruit of arduous mid-winter weaving,
given away in a morning,
brings no relief from great hunger;
famished children in a line like bamboo stalks.
I look back to younger, more sprightly days
when I knew nothing of the affairs of the world.
For a man who has read thousands of books,
passing the government examination, I thought,
would be like pulling a hair from my beard.
I was filled with sudden self-conceit;
surely a good post will be allotted me.
Why have I had such a mediocre lot,
why has poverty embraced my sad path?
Reflecting sincerely on all this,
obviously I'm not without fault.
In my drinking, I never had control;
invariably I tipped a thousand cups.
Words normally kept hidden in my heart
under wine's influence were not kept back.
I didn't stop till I had spewed everything out,
little knowing how false charges and vilification follow.
My conduct uniformly thus,
I deserved all this poverty and hunger.
Those beneath me did not like me;
heaven above denied me its protection.
Wherever I went, things got fouled up;
whatever I did turned out wrong.

All my own doing.
Sad, but who can I blame?
I counted my sins on my fingers
and gave myself three lashes of the whip.
But what's the point in repenting the past?
What I have to do is improve the future.

ONE DAY IN THE FIFTH MONTH OF THE YEAR OF *KIMI*, A THOUSAND
POMEGRANATE FLOWERS BLOOMED IN CH'OE CH'UNGHŎN'S HOUSE:
HE SUMMONED ME TO COMPOSE A POEM (*hanshi*)

After Ch'oe Ch'unghŏn (1149–1219) established his new order in 1196, he wielded su-
preme power in Koryŏ. He and his family virtually ruled the kingdom for several genera-
tions. Although he was a dictator, he won the hearts of the people by the reforms he intro-
duced in land ownership, taxation, and the treatment of peasants and slaves.

The first flush of wine is on jade faces;
a pink tint invades their world.
Petal folds are like fairy wings;
beauty beguiles the guests' souls.
Fresh, fragrant days entice the butterflies;
nights of exploding light awe the birds.
Beauty so prized it's bid bloom late;
who can understand the heart of the Creator?

THE GOVERNOR TO THE ELDERS (*hanshi*)
I am an old scholar;
I won't call myself governor.
Thus I present myself to the elders.
Think of me as an old farmer, I say.
If you have a grievance, come and make your case,
like a child looking for mother's milk.
The drought continues; heaven sends no rain;
this, too, is my responsibility.
I apologize sincerely to all the elders.
I think I should resign without delay.
You'll be better off if I go;
where's the point in holding on to an old man like me?

THE ELDERS' REPLY TO THE GOVERNOR (*hanshi*)

The sweet pear reference is to a poem in the Book of Songs. *The people of Zhou so revered the memory of Shao Bao's wise government that they treasured an old pear tree under which he once rested. The people are asking Yi Kyubo to be another Shao Bao for them.*

Excellency, your impatience with us
prompts you to resign your post.
Our village land may be barren,
but the natural features
are as strong as a dragon.
Official appointees to the village
receive the royal summons within a matter of months.
We beseech you, excellency, bear with us a while.
Take a rest beneath the sweet pear tree.
An emissary will surely come from the nine-gate palace
to escort you to the royal presence.

THOUGHTS ON EYES GROWING DIM: PRESENTED TO CHŎN IJI
(*hanshi*)

I'm forty-four now;
both eyes are beginning to blur.
I can't distinguish people even at very close range;
it's as if a dense spring mist were blocking the view.
I consulted a physician. The physician said:
your liver is the problem, it's not what it should be:
or perhaps when you were young
you read too much in the shadow of the lamp.
Hearing this, I clapped my hands and laughed outright.
You're not a very skilled physician, I said.
People with ears want to hear;
those who can't hear are deaf.
People with eyes want to see;
those who can't see are blind.
I wanted to see the king,
but I had no access to the nine-gate palace.
I wanted to see men of rank in ceremonial cloth of gold,
but dressed in hemp I couldn't conceal my presence.

I wanted to see the peonies,
but only useless weeds grew verdant.
I never lived in a first-rate house;
in a hut in a mugwort field my hair turned white.
I never ate fine ceremonial food;
many's the time I missed a meal.
That's why my eyes are dim,
that's why they're bothering me as if veiled in hemp.
This is all the decree of heaven;
I can't cure it with medicine.
Who knows, it may turn out to be a blessing;
I may finish my days deaf and blind.

SEVENTH MONTH, TENTH DAY: I SANG OF MY FEELINGS AT DAWN
AND SHOWED THE POEM TO TONGGOJA (*hanshi*)
Tonggoja (Pak Hwan'go) was a close friend of Yi Kyubo.

A poet is a man of innate sensibility:
he marvels at autumn in a single leaf,
and though summer heat is still around,
he thinks of warm fur at the approach of dawn.
Yesterday he bathed in South Stream;
he swam like a seagull in the water.
Today he looks at those same blue waters;
already cold currents make him balk.
The seasons change a day at a time;
time never pauses in its flow.
Tomorrow is not today;
black heads change to white.
Life is a brief lodging,
a hundred years at most.
Why be a rat, head stretched out of the hole,
unable to decide on direction?
Small hearts either encompass great pain
or, harnessing effort to will,
spit on their hands and grab a title.
The alternative is to return to origins,

to sit in the fields and devote oneself to farming.
One hundred measures of wine brewed every year
guarantee old age on wine's hill.
When it comes to death and becoming clay under a pine,
life is the same for low and high.

WRITTEN ON THE WALL WITH FLYING BRUSH, USING ONCE
AGAIN A RHYME FROM ONE OF THE ANCIENTS (*hanshi*)
The moon stands out against the gelid blue of sky after the rain has
    cleared.
I can almost hear the raindrops fall from the twelve painted lotus
    blossoms.
There's nothing to do except burn incense.
Now at last I realize the nobility of the monk's calling.

THANKS TO A FRIEND FOR SENDING WINE (*hanshi*)
These days the wine cup has run dry;
a drought has stricken this house.
Thanks for your present of fragrant wine;
it's as pleasurable as rain at the proper time.

GRIEVING FOR MY LITTLE GIRL (*hanshi*)
My little girl's face was white as snow;
I can't tell you how bright and intelligent she was.
She was talking by the time she was two,
her tongue more plastic than a parrot.
At three she became girl conscious, reserved;
she didn't go outside the gate to play.
This year she was four; already she was good at sewing.
How could she be deprived of life, how could she be gone to the other
    world?
It was all so sudden it's unreal:
a nestling fallen to the ground before it could grow,
a terrible indictment of her father's home.
I am acquainted with the Way;
I can bear my pain to a point,
but the tears of my wife, when will they end?

I look at that field:
new shoots beset by unseasonable wind and hail
face certain destruction.
The Creator put her here;
the Creator just as suddenly snatched her away.
What happens in this world is all subterfuge;
life's comings and goings are illusory.
It's all over now; go in peace to your eternal rest.

COMING HOME DRUNK FROM THE TEMPLE OF CALM AND PEACE
(hanshi)

Wang Kŏn (the founder of Koryŏ, r. 918–943) built Anhwa-sa Temple on the slopes of Song'ak san in Kaesŏng in memory of his younger brother, who was taken as a hostage to Latter Paekche. He also built ten temples within Kaesŏng to commemorate the founding of Koryŏ, one of which was called Anhwa-sa. It was a small palace noted for its scenic beauty; the king often resided there.

Sozzled drunk in Yoni Pavilion;
I came home at night along the rough, stony road.
I went at my leisure, early, alone;
the moon was so bright it brought two of us home.

ON POETRY (hanshi)
Writing poetry is a consummate art:
expression and thought form a lovely harmony.
When thought's significance is truly deep
the flavor improves with every chew.
Deep thought without smooth expression
makes for coarse texture; the unfolding of meaning is precluded.
Decorating and chiseling for embellishment
are of secondary importance,
and yet it takes a supreme effort
to reject a fine line not quite to the point.
To grab the flower and abandon the fruit
causes the poem to lose real meaning.
Today's crop of poets ignore
the profound worth of the *Book of Songs*.

They decorate the skin colorfully;
they follow the fashion of the moment.
Meaning is postulated in heaven;
it is hard to get it right.
Aware of this difficulty,
they are content to decorate the exterior.
Thus they try to dazzle the crowd,
to conceal the absence of deep thought.
With the gradual development of this trend
good writing has been knocked to the ground.
Li Bai and Du Fu are not coming back;
on whose authority am I to sort the true from the false?
I want to repair the broken base of letters,
but there's no one to carry a basket of earth.
I can recite three hundred verses from the *Book of Songs*;
whom can I satirize, whom can I help?
All I can do is do what I can.
I cry alone: others laugh me to scorn.

VISITED A FRIEND IN THE SNOW BUT DID NOT MEET HIM *(hanshi)*
Cha *meant the name given to a youth when he reached adulthood, wore his topknot up, and donned his formal hat. He was most commonly known by this name for the rest of his life.*

The snow shines whiter than paper;
I take my whip and write my name and *cha*.
Don't let the wind sweep the spot;
kindly wait for the master to come.

AN OLD *KISAENG* *(hanshi)*
Face once lovely, now a flower-fallen branch;
who can see the alluring fifteen-year-old you once were?
Song and dance are as beguiling as of old.
I am touched: your skills have not faded at all.

SHIJO 1730
This is the only extant Yi Kyubo shijo; the attribution, however, is doubtful.

Warm weather, gentle breezes;
birds twitter in song.
I lie at leisure on a blanket of fallen leaves.
Today
my mountain home reposes in peace.

CHIN HWA, THIRTEENTH CENTURY

Chin Hwa is listed with Yi Kyubo in "Hallim pyŏlgok" for his excellence in writing extempore rhyming couplets. We do not have precise dates, but we know he passed the civil service examination in 1200 and built a reputation for himself as an outstanding poet.

THE FIFTH WATCH *(hanshi)*
I knew nothing of the fierce wind and rain of the Fifth Watch.
Bound in mellow, tipsy dreams, I missed the crowing of the cock.
"The stream in front is flooded," the boy suddenly cried.
Half of yesterday's crop of mountain flowers already lines the stone
    steps.

WAITING FOR THE LIGHT *(hanshi)*
China to the west is in a sorry state;
the frontier north is confusion personified.
I sit and await the burgeoning of the light;
the sun tries to redden in the eastern sky.

WALKING THROUGH THE FIELDS *(hanshi)*
Tiny plum petals fall; willows dance a dizzy dance.
I tread the blue force, step by measured step.
The door of the fish shop is closed; voices are few.
Spring rain decks the river with whirls of blue thread.

HYESHIM (NATIONAL PRECEPTOR CHIN'GAK), 1178–1234

Hyeshim was born in Naju in Chŏlla Province. His real name was Ch'oe Shik; his pen name, Muŭija, literally means the man with no clothes. He wanted to leave home after the death of his father, Ch'oe Wan, but his mother prevailed upon him to pursue formal study and enter officialdom. After his mother's death, he became a disciple of Chinŭl, National Preceptor Pojo. Upon the death of Chinŭl in 1210, Hyeshim was appointed as head monk of Susŏn-sa (today's Songgwang-sa). He contributed greatly to the development of Zen philosophy.

THE DAY THE MASTER DIED (*hanshi*)

The dead master is Chinŭl (1158–1210), a pivotal figure in the reform of Korea's Buddhist tradition, who emphasized Zen meditation as the way to salvation. He was the founder of the Chogye tradition, Korea's main Buddhist sect to the present day. Shaolin Temple (Sorim-sa in Korean) is where Bodhidharma lodged when he came from India. Salvation, he said, could not be attained through good works. He spent nine years looking at a wall in meditation. Zen traces its roots here.

Mid-spring—the hermitage is crystal clean—not a mote;
flower petals spot the green moss.
Who said all news from Shaolin Temple is cut off?
At the perfect moment the evening breeze sends a subtle flower
    fragrance.

SMALL LOTUS POND (*hanshi*)

No wind, no swell;
a world so various opens before my eyes.
No need for a lot of words;
to look is to see.

ENJOYED A SPRING DAY IN SPARROW VALLEY TEMPLE:
PRESENTED TO THE OLD HEAD MONK (*hanshi*)

Yŏn'gok-sa (Sparow Valley Temple) is at the entrance to Chiri san (Mount Chiri) in Chŏlla. The Main Hall boasts a lotus pond in front, from which sparrows were supposed to fly. Destroyed during the Hideyoshi Wars, it was restored in 1627.

Mid-spring; the old hermitage was quiet, no pressing affairs.
Wind down, flower petals covered the front step.
I was enjoying the evening glow and the clear clouds
when the scops owl's cry disturbed the mountain.

LOOKING AT A SHADOW (*hanshi*)

I'm sitting alone at the edge of the pond;
I see a monk at the bottom of the water.

We observe each other with a quiet smile.
I know you, I say! He doesn't answer.

COMPOSED ON MYOGO TERRACE (*hanshi*)
Myogo Terrace literally means lovely-high-terrace.

The clouds at leisure on the top of the pass are not about to lift.
Why is the stream in such a rush?
I pick pine-nuts under the pines;
they complement the fragrance of the drawing tea.

AFTER RAIN (*hanshi*)
Strange bird calls echo through the deep valley;
patches of white cloud pattern the blue mountain.
I sit here quietly after the rain; I have nothing to do;
The clouds may be impassive, but the birds never rest.

BESIDE THE WATER (*hanshi*)
I chanced on clear waters and looked therein.
I was shocked to see the frost and snow that covered my head.
I've never worried about the world or personal affairs.
Who cultivated all this white hair?

NEAR MOON TERRACE (*hanshi*)
The cliff face soars countless feet;
the high terrace on top stretches close to the sky.
The Great Dipper scoops water from the Milky Way
     to brew a pot of tea at night.
The steam from the teapot coldly wraps the cassia tree on the moon.

MOUNTAIN DIVERSION (*hanshi*)
From the bank of the stream I wash my feet;
I cleanse my eyes by looking at the mountain.
I entertain no idle dreams of fame and honor.
What else need I do?

HONORABLE BAMBOO (*hanshi*)
I love the honorable bamboo
because it beats both cold and heat.
The older it gets, the more upright it is;
the more time goes by, the more it empties the heart.
Its games are crystal in moonlight;
it sends its words on the wind.
Snow crowned,
it is a manly presence in the woods.

CH'OE HANG, ?—1257

Ch'oe Hang, grandson of General Ch'oe Ch'unghŏn, chose the life of a monk because he was the child of a kisaeng. Persuaded by his father, Ch'oe I (?—1249), to return to the world, he became an official in the Koryŏ court. He was noted for his uncompromising policies in dealing with the Mongols.

QUATRAIN (*hanshi*)
The kŏmun'go is a traditional Korean stringed instrument.

Moonlight filling the yard is a smokeless candle;
Mountain shade obtruding is an unexpected guest.
The pine *kŏmun'go* plays an unnotated melody.
All this with prudence, please, lest others find out.

CH'UNGJI (NATIONAL PRECEPTOR WŎN'GAM), 1226—1292

National Preceptor Wŏn'gam was from Changhŭng in Chŏlla. His Buddhist name was Ch'ungji. At the age of nineteen, he took first place in the civil service examination. As an envoy to Japan, he made a name for himself for his superior writing style. He resigned from public life, became a monk, and was a disciple of Ch'ŏnyŏng (National Preceptor Wŏno, 1215—1286).

AT LEISURE: MEDLEY (*hanshi*)
I raise the glass bead curtain, embrace the mountain light.
The bamboo water-run shares the gurgling stream.
Throughout the morning few people seek me out;
the cuckoo calls his name.

ABOUT MYSELF (*hanshi*)

Already my time has slipped by;
old age and sickness are friends; we lean on each other.
I've no strength in my legs, they depend on the cane;
my body is so emaciated, I've taken in my belt.
With a full belly and nothing to do, I've become lazy;
with wisdom as my daily fare, I don't put on weight.
When the sun goes down I wash some coarse rice.
It's late spring, but I still wear quilted clothes.
Because I live so poorly I have few monk friends.
And the city is so far away I've even fewer friends on the outside.
All I have for friends are the lonely clouds;
from time to time they seek me out under the eaves.

DEATH SONG (*hanshi*)

*This was written by Kim Hun on Wŏn'gam's monument. Tradition says that Wŏn'gam
prepared carefully for death. Having shaved his head, bathed, and changed his clothes, he
informed his disciples that life and death are part of this world and that it was time for him
to depart. He sat in the meditation position, recited this death song, and took his leave.*

Sixty-seven years have passed;
all is consummated this morning.
The road home is smooth;
I won't lose my way.
My staff may be all I carry,
but thankfully my legs won't tire on the way.

SLEPT IN BEGINNING OF PEACE TEMPLE ON THE TWENTY-FOURTH
DAY OF THE THIRD MONTH (*hanshi*)

*Kaet'ae-sa (Beginning of Peace Temple) was built in 936 on Ch'ŏnho san (Heavenly
Protector Mountain) by the founder of Koryŏ, Wang Kŏn (r. 918–943), to celebrate his
victory over Latter Paekche and the unification of the country.*

I pass the temple on Ch'ŏnho san three times a year.
The white clouds that blanket the mountain are truly white.
Those white clouds boast of mountain leisure;
they mock the wayfarer who leaves.

White clouds! Don't mock me, I say;
my steps are neither right nor wrong.
How did you know I wouldn't put down roots in another mountain,
that I'd come back here to play with you?

U T'AK, 1263–1342

U T'ak was a scholar-official during the Koryŏ dynasty. He retired early from the court because of palace scandals, which he uncovered in the course of his official duties. He devoted the rest of his life to scholarly pursuits.

SHIJO 2060

The breeze that melted the blue mountain snow
blew suddenly and was gone.
I'll borrow that breeze a moment and blow it across my head,
to melt
the frost lodged so long in these locks.

SHIJO 2270

In one hand I grasped a bramble,
in the other I held a stick:
the bramble to block the advance of age, the stick to stay approaching
    white hair.
White hair, though,
outwitted me: it took a shortcut here.

YI CHO'NYŎN, 1269–1343

Yi Cho'nyŏn was a scholar-statesman who visited the Yuan court in Beijing several times as an envoy of the Koryŏ kings. The poem below may have been written on one such visit. Composed almost entirely in Chinese characters, it presents some difficulty to the translator. The third line reads literally: "One branch [tree] spring heart how can the cuckoo know?"

The description is highly symbolic and may refer to the poet's sweetheart, the king, or the country. Alternatively the poem may be taken as a sigh for the sad days that have come to the Koryŏ kingdom. In old Korea the night was divided into five watches, the third being the hour immediately before and after midnight.

Moonlight white on white pear blossoms;
the Milky Way in the Third Watch.
How could the cuckoo know that spring suffuses the branch?
Love, too,
is like a sickness; I cannot sleep tonight.

YI CHEHYŎN, 1287–1367

Yi Chehyŏn, a scholar-official in Koryŏ and a leading exponent of neo-Confucian phi-
losophy, was one of the great poets of the age. Self-cultivation was his goal. Every experi-
ence came as a fresh challenge to sensibility. He held a succession of high-ranking posts at
court before being sent into exile for purportedly conspiring against the king. His innocence
was soon established, however, and he returned to court to resume his official career. He ac-
companied several embassies to China and spent more than twenty years in Beijing, where
he was the undisputed Korean master of Chinese language and literature.

SNOWY NIGHT IN THE MOUNTAINS (*hanshi*)
"Squall" means the novice's complaints when the open door lets in the cold.

The quilt is paper; I'm cold, and the worship hall lantern is dim.
The young novice rings no bell throughout the night.
A guest opening the door so early is in for a squall,
but I've got to see the snow weighing down the pine outside the
    hermitage.

PODŎK CAVE (*hanshi*)
Podŏk Cave on Paekdu san (Mount Paekdu) in North Korea had a floor of stones, un-
der which the tinkling water flowed.

A chill wind blows between the rocks;
the stream is so deep its blue is enhanced.
Stick in hand I look at the cliff;
the eaves fly into the clouds.

ANCIENT PORTRAIT (*hanshi*)
Years ago, when this portrait was painted,
my sideburns had the dark luster of spring.

How long has this painting been doing the rounds?
I look at it again; everything is as it was.
Substance hasn't changed;
former self and later self are one.
My grandchildren don't recognize me;
"Who is it?" they ask.

TWILIGHT IN A FISHING VILLAGE (*hanshi*)
The twilight sun is about to sink among distant peaks;
The homing tide gurgles as it climbs the gelid shore.
Fishermen disappear among the flowering reeds;
smoke from cooking fires is even bluer in the fading light.

ENDANGERED TREASURE (*soak pu*)
This poem belongs to a genre called soak pu, *translations of popular Korean vernacular poems into Chinese. The original title, "Chewibo," refers to a state organization devoted to helping the destitute. Koryŏ sa (History of Koryŏ) tells of a young lady in the Chewibo who was unable to deal with her shame when a young gallant took her hand. The interpretation of Yi Chehyŏn's poem seems quite the opposite.*

I was washing my silks by the willow stream
when a gentleman on a white horse took my hand and spoke of love.
For three months the rain has dripped from the eaves.
How can I wash the lingering fragrance from my fingertips?

NEW YEAR'S DAY: YEAR OF THE DOG (*hanshi*)
Whenever I see a white-haired old man with a stick on the road,
I say to myself: "When I'm old, I won't go out."
What a laugh! Already I'm seventy-two;
cockcrow, and I'm on my horse for a round of New Year's greetings.

NO SECOND THOUGHT (*hanshi*)
The desire for fame and honor fades with the advance of age.
I want to spend my last years with a certain poise;
to cut reeds at the water's side, to watch cloud shadows,
to move the plantain under the window, and to listen to the patter
    of the rain.

REMEMBERING SONGDO—EIGHT SONGS (2):
LATE AUTUMN ON DRAGON MOUNTAIN (*hanshi*)
Songdo (modern Kaesŏng) was the capital of Koryŏ.

Last year when the chrysanthemums bloomed on Dragon Mountain,
I took a guest and a jug of wine up the slope.
My hat flew off in a gust of pine wind;
we came home drunk, our clothes covered in red leaves.

REMEMBERING SONGDO—EIGHT SONGS (8):
BOATING IN THE MOONLIGHT ON WEST RIVER (*hanshi*)
The river is cold; the night is quiet; fish are slow to take.
I sit alone on the side of the boat, pulling in the line.
Blue mountains fill my eyes; moonlight fills the boat.
You don't need a beauty for "flowing wind" elegance.

INVITATION TO CH'OE HAE, AN OLD FRIEND (*hanshi*)
*Ch'oe Hae (1287–1340), a scholar-official at the end of Koryŏ, was born in Yesan and
wrote poetry from an early age. He was direct and unbending and made quite a few ene-
mies as a result, so his progress in the bureaucracy was effectively blocked. Yi Chehyŏn's
poem shows that Cho'e Hae's personality had a softer side.*

Kŏmun'go, books, and a grass-roof hut:
I lie here alone savoring the exquisite flavor.
Won't you come and visit?
My eastside neighbor's wine has matured.

KUYO DANG 2 (*hanshi*)
*Kuyo dang (literally, nine-light hall) was a Taoist shrine in which various rituals were
performed. The king prayed for rain here, and royal betrothal ceremonies were carried out.
The shrine disappeared when Chosŏn was set up.*

I waken from dreams; moonlight filtering through the window half fills
   the room.
A bell tolls in the woods: it's from the monk's house, I know.
Suddenly there's an edge to the dawn breeze.
In the morning there are flower petals in the stream flowing south.

CH'OE SARIP, ?—?

No dates are available for Ch'oe Sarip. His poem has all the marks of Koryŏ, however: it is passionate and uninhibited. When Chosŏn gentlemen made a similar mistake, their big worry was that they would become a laughing-stock.

WAITING (*hanshi*)
I put down the wine jar in front of Long Life Gate.
Willow branches fly in the wind as I wait for my love.
My gaze is steady as the sun slants across a distant peak.
I feel sure it's she, but when she nears I know it's not.

CHŎNG P'O, 1309—1345

Chŏng P'o was a scholar-official during the reign of Ch'unghye (1315–1344) of Koryŏ. Skilled in poetry and calligraphy, he belonged to the new elite (sadaebu) that came to power toward the end of the dynasty.

PARTING FROM MY LOVE IN YANGJU INN (*hanshi*)
The dawn candle lights up what's left of her makeup.
Good-bye is so difficult to say; already there's numbness in the gut.
We push the door open; the waning moon is dim in the
     middle of the yard;
pale apricot shadows suffuse our clothes.

CH'OE YŎNG, 1316—1388

Ch'oe Yŏng was general of the army in the last days of Koryŏ. He had a brilliant military career, putting down several internal rebellions and repeatedly repulsing the invasions of Japanese pirates. In 1388 he was defeated in battle by his bitter rival Yi Sŏnggye, founder of the Chosŏn dynasty. Ch'oe was exiled and eventually killed. The song below reflects the courage, loyalty, and indomitable will of the old warrior.

SHIJO 516
Don't laugh at an old pine
for bending under the weight of snow.
Do spring breeze blossoms stay beautiful forever?
When snowflakes
fly in the wind, it's you who'll envy me.

HYEGŬN, 1320—1376

Hyegŭn was a Koryŏ monk who studied meditation in China. He returned to Koryŏ
in 1371 and became royal preceptor under King Kongmin.

THE WAY (*hanshi*)

It's never been possible to fabricate nature.
Why do I look for enlightenment outside?
All I know for truth is that there's no action in the heart.
Thirsty, I brew tea; tired, I take a nap.

YI SAEK, 1328—1396

Yi Saek was a scholar-official who was on friendly terms with Yi Sŏnggye and his group
but refused to support the new dynasty. He was sent into exile after the murder of Chŏng
Mongju. Yi Sŏnggye, recognizing his abilities, asked him to work for the new dynasty, but
he refused. Yi Saek expressed his disenchantment by retiring to the country, where he was
known as Mogŭn or Hiding Cowherd.

SONG OF A MADMAN (*hanshi*)

I'm the quiet type; turmoil is not my thing;
only a cloud on the wind is in constant motion.
I'm the open type; I don't have hidden agendas;
water in a well cannot flow.
Water, in reflecting an object, shows the beautiful and the ugly;
clouds are insensible; they gather and scatter at will.
When I see heaven's will in nature,
how can I let time pass idly by?
When I have money, I buy wine. No need for second thoughts.
When I have wine, I want flowers. Why hesitate?
I look at the flowers, drink the wine, let my white hair stream free;
I climb East Mountain, enjoy the moon and the breeze.

FEELINGS ON LOOKING AT CHRYSANTHEMUMS (*hanshi*)

The poem refers to Tao Yuanming's transcendence upon looking at the chrysanthe-
mums that adorned his eastern fence.

Can human caring be as heartless as material things?
The longer the relationship, the less secure you feel.

I look at the fence to the east; my face is red with embarrassment.
In front of genuine yellow chrysanthemums, I feel I'm a sham Tao
    Yuanming.

SHIJO 890

The plum is a traditional symbol of loyalty. The melting snow perhaps represents the
waning Koryŏ dynasty, threatened by hostile forces symbolized here by the thick clouds.
Scholarly interpretations of the text differ, however. Not all agree that the snow is melting;
some maintain that the verb modifier means continuously falling, while others say that it
refers to a thick carpet of snow.

Clouds cluster thick
where white snow melts in the valley.
The lovely plum, where has it bloomed?
I stand alone
in the setting sun, not knowing whither I should go.

CHO UNHŬL, 1332–1404

Cho Unhŭl was prime minister of Koryŏ. While staying in the country to avoid possible
repercussions from a purge, he noticed a group of court officials who were crossing the river
on their way into exile and wrote a poem to record the event. He seems to have been a very
colorful character, noted for his easy, humorous personality. When he was living as a her-
mit near Sangju, he rode an ox in and out of his mountain retreat.

IMPROMPTU (*hanshi*)
The heat of the day was too much to bear;
I called the lad to open the brushwood gate.
I walked as far as the pavilion in the forest and sat on a mossy stone.
Last night in the mountains the wind and rain were fierce; blossoms fill
    the swirling water.

YI CHIK, 1362–1431

Yi Chik was one of the Koryŏ ministers who helped Yi Sŏnggye in the government of the
new Chosŏn dynasty. He held a number of offices, including prime minister. In the third
year of the reign of T'aejong, he supervised the making of the first movable metal type. Some
commentators point out that the poem below reflects his pangs of conscience for supporting
Yi Sŏnggye.

White heron, do not mock
the crow for being black.
Black outside, is it black inside, too?
White outside,
black inside: that's really you.

YI PANG'WŎN (T'AEJONG), 1367—1422

Yi Pang'wŏn, the fifth son of General Yi Sŏnggye, was a pivotal figure in the plot to overthrow the Koryŏ dynasty and establish his father as the first king of the Chosŏn dynasty. Yi Pang'wŏn became the third king of the dynasty; he is known to history as T'aejong.

HAYŎ KA (SONG OF IMPONDERABLES): *SHIJO* 1641

While contemplating the overthrow of the Koryŏ dynasty, the story goes, Yi Pang'wŏn gave a reception to which all the key political figures of the day were invited. Among them was Chŏng Mongju, a man renowned for his unshakable loyalty to the Koryŏ kings. Yi Pang'wŏn is said to have sung the following poem to Chŏng Mongju in order to observe his reaction to a proffered alliance. Mansu san (literally, long-life-mountain) is outside the west gate of Songdo (Kaesŏng), the old capital of Koryŏ. The authenticity of the ascription of the poem is doubted by some.

What about living this way?
What about living that way?
What about arrowroot vines intertwining on Mansu san?
Intertwined,
we, too, could spend a hundred years in joy.

CHŎNG MONGJU, 1337—1392

Chŏng Mongju's response to Yi Pang'wŏn's proposed alliance was unequivocal.

The poem has added poignancy because supporters of Yi Pang'wŏn murdered Chŏng Mongju shortly afterward. Tradition has it that Chŏng was aware of imminent death. Out of respect for his parents, who had given him life, he thought it would lack decorum to be other than drunk for the occasion. Accordingly, he consumed a large amount of wine before setting out to face death. Tradition tells us that he mounted his horse back to front, because he felt it would be unbecoming to see the fatal blow. Thus he never saw the iron club that felled him as he crossed Sŏnjuk (Straight Bamboo) Bridge. A bamboo tree (a tradi-

tional symbol for unswerving moral probity) is said to have grown on the spot; the stonework of the bridge is speckled red, which some like to regard as the blood of the hero. Again the authenticity of the ascription of the poem is in doubt.

TANSHIM KA (SONG OF A RED-BLOODED HEART)

Though my body die and die again,
though it die a hundred deaths,
my skeleton turn to dust, my soul exist or not,
could the heart change
that's red-blooded in undivided loyalty to its lord?

KANGNAM SONG (*hanshi*)

A Kangnam girl, flower pinned in her hair,
smiles and calls her lover to sport on the grassy bank.
I punt home in the fading light.
Mandarin ducks fly in pairs; my cares are limitless.

SPRING MOOD (*hanshi*)

Spring rain too fine for drops to form;
just a hint of sound in the night.
Melting snow fills South Stream;
I'll bet new grass is popping up.

CHŎNG MONGJU'S MOTHER, ?—?

Kagok wŏllyu attributes this poem to Chŏng Mongju's mother, but the ascription is doubtful.

SHIJO 18

One traditional interpretation of the poem sees it as a mother's warning to her son destined for greatness, telling him to be careful how he comports himself. A second interpretation sees the warning as more specific, referring to the famous banquet hosted by Yi Pang'wŏn. "Clear water" is a reference to a river in ancient China wherein loyal ministers washed their ears whenever they were tempted by the lures of power and ambition.

White heron, do not go
where crows squabble.
Angry crows resent your whiteness.

Clean now,
washed in clear water, your body, I fear, may be sullied.

YI CHONO, 1341–1371

Yi Chono was an official in the Koryŏ court. He incurred the wrath of King Kongmin by writing a memorial to the throne deploring the purportedly violent acts of Shin Ton (?–1371), a monk who was extremely powerful at court. Yi Chono escaped severe punishment through the intercession of Yi Saek, but he was demoted. He retired and spent the rest of his life in seclusion.

SHIJO 224

The clouds refer to Shin Ton: they are responsible for their actions when they block the light of the sun (the king). Shin Ton was born a slave, became a monk, and rose to high position in King Kongmin's government. Entrusted with putting Kongmin's reforms into effect, he took land from rich landowners and gave it to peasants. He also freed the slaves. The landowners reacted fiercely, calling him treasonous. He was sent into exile and killed within a few days. Shin Ton was accused of arrogance, immoral conduct, trying to move the capital, and causing confusion in the king's mind. These charges are recorded by the aristocrats who toppled him from power, however, and hence are not very credible. Historians today take a much less jaundiced view of Shin Ton's activities.

To say the clouds are unwitting
is a groundless fabrication.
High in the sky they ride, at liberty to go wherever they desire.
Why on earth
do they follow the sun and shade its dazzling light?

CHŎNG TOJŎN, 1342–1398

Chŏng Tojŏn was a pivotal figure in the reform group that helped General Yi Sŏnggye to found the new Chosŏn dynasty; he rose to high office in the government. He helped give the reform policies of the new government a Confucian ideological basis. General Yi's son, Yi Pang'wŏn, murdered him in a purge directed at his own half-brothers, one of whom was the crown prince and in Chŏng Tojŏn's care.

HOEGO KA (SONG OF THE PAST)

Immortals' Bridge was in Songdo (Kaesŏng), the Koryŏ capital; Chahadong was a village nestling on the lower slopes of Song'ak san (Pine Ridge Mountain) near Songdo.

The water under Immortals' Bridge
flows all the way to Chahadong,
the sound all that remains of five hundred years of Koryŏ.
Boy,
there's no point in asking about the rise and fall of nations that are
    gone.

YI SŬNGIN, 1349–1392

Yi Sŭngin was a scholar-official. He incurred the enmity of Chŏng Tojŏn, a powerful bureaucrat, and was murdered by one of Chŏng's men.

THE MONK'S HUT (*hanshi*)

Mountains to the north, mountains to the south; the narrow track forks.
Pine pollen, wet with rain, falls pell-mell.
The hermit draws water and returns to his straw hut.
A plume of blue smoke dyes the white clouds.

BIBLIOGRAPHY

PRE-SHILLA SONGS

Cho Tongil. *Han'guk munhak t'ongsa*. Seoul: Chishik sanŏpsa, 1989.

Hŏ Kyŏngjin, compiler. *Uri yetshi*. Seoul: Ch'onga ch'ulp'ansa, 1986.

Hoyt, James. *Soaring Phoenixes and Prancing Dragons*. Somerset, N.J.: Jimoondang, 2000.

Hyŏngnyŏn Chŏng. *Kyunyŏ chŏn*. Translated by Adrian Buzo and Tony Price (*Kyunyŏ Chŏn: The Life and Songs of a Tenth-Century Korean Monk*). New South Wales, Australia: Wild Peony, 1993.

Iryŏn. *Samguk yusa*. Translated by Ha Taehŭng and Graham K. Mintz. Seoul: Yŏnsei University Press, 1972.

Kim Chonggil and Lee Ŏryŏng, editors. *Uriŭi myŏngshi*. Seoul: Tonga ch'ulp'ansa, 1990.

Kim Yong, compiler. *Uri kojŏn shiga hanmadang*. Seoul: Hyemun sŏgwan, 1994.

SHILLA *HYANGGA*

Chang Chinha. *Shilla hyanggaui yŏn'gu*. Seoul: Hyŏngsŏl ch'ulp'ansa, 1996.

Cho Tongil. *Han'guk munhak t'ongsa*. Seoul: Chishik sanŏpsa, 1989.

Hoyt, James. *Soaring Phoenixes and Prancing Dragons*. Somerset, N.J.: Jimoondang, 2000.

Iryŏn. *Samguk yusa*. Translated by Ha Taehŭng and Graham K. Mintz. Seoul: Yŏnsei University Press, 1972.

Kang Kil'un. *Hyangga Shin haedok yŏn'gu*. Seoul: Hangmun sa, 1995.

Kim Hŭnggyu. *Understanding Korean Literature*. Translated by Robert J. Fouser. New York: Sharpe, 1997.

Kim Sangson. *Han'guk shiga hyŏngt'aeron*. Seoul: Ilchogak, 1979.

Kim Wanjin. *Hyangga haedokpŏp yŏn'gu*. Seoul: Seoul University Press, 1980.

Kim Yong, compiler. *Uri kojŏn shiga hanmadang*. Seoul: Hyemun sŏgwan, 1994.

Lee Ŏryŏng. *Kojŏnul ilgnŭn pŏp*. Seoul: Kabin ch'ulp'ansa, 1985.

Lee, Peter H. *Korean Literature: Topics and Themes*. Tucson: University of Arizona Press, 1965.

Ogura Shimpei. *Hyangga mit iduŭi yŏn'gu*. Seoul: Kyŏngsŏng cheguk taehak, 1929.

Paek Yong and Chŏng Pyŏng'uk, editors. *Han'guk kojŏn shiga chakp'umnon*. Seoul: Chimmundang, 1992.

Yang Chudong. *Koga yŏn'gu*. Seoul: Pangmun sŏgwan, 1942.

KORYŎ *KAYO*

Akchang kasa. Thought to have been edited by Pak Chun during the Chungjong-Myŏngjong era (sixteenth century). The author and date cannot be determined with accuracy.

Akhak kwebŏm. Compiled and edited in 1493. Reissued in 1610 by Yi Chŏnggu et al. This reissue is in the National Archives (Kyujanggak).

Ch'oe Mijŏng. *Koryŏ sokyoui chŏnsŭng yŏn'gu*. Seoul: Kyemyŏng University Press, 1999.

Cho Kyuik. *Koryŏ sokak kasa, kyŏnggich'e ka, sonch'o akchang*. Seoul: Hansaem ch'ulp'an chushik hoesa, 1993.

Cho Tongil. *Han'guk munhak t'ongsa*. Seoul: Chishik sanŏpsa, 1989.

Hoyt, James. *Soaring Phoenixes and Prancing Dragons*. Somerset, N.J.: Jimoondang, 2000.

Iryŏn. *Samguk yusa*. Translated by Ha Taehŭng and Graham K. Mintz. Seoul: Yŏnsei University Press, 1972.

Kim Hŭnggyu. *Understanding Korean Literature*. Translated by Robert J. Fouser. New York: Sharpe, 1987.

Kim Sangsŏn. *Han'guk shiga hyŏngt'aeron*. Seoul: Ilchogak, 1979.

Kim Yong, compiler. *Uri kojŏn shiga hanmadang*. Seoul: Hyemun sŏgwan, 1994.

Lee, Peter H. *Korean Literature: Topics and Themes*. Tucson: University of Arizona Press. 1965.

O'Rourke, Kevin. *A Hundred Love Poems from Old Korea*. Folkestone: Global Oriental, 2005.

Paek Yong and Chŏng Pyŏng'uk, editors. *Han'guk kojŏn shiga chakp'umnon*. Seoul: Chimmundang, 1992.

Pak Pyŏngch'ae. *Koryŏ kayoŭi ŏsŏk yŏn'gu*. Seoul: Kukhak charyo wŏn, 1994.

Shiyong hyangakpo. Editor and date not established. Presumably written in the reign of Chungjong-Myŏngjong or perhaps Sŏnjo (sixteenth and early seventeenth century). Part of the collection of Yi Kyŏmno.

HANSHI

Chŏng Chongdae. *Han'guk hanshi sogŭi salmgwa ŭishik.* Seoul: Saemun sa, 2005.

Hŏ Kyŏngjin. *Han'gukŭi hanshi.* Seoul: P'yŏngmin sa, multivolume series from 1986.

————, compiler. *Uri yetshi.* Seoul: Ch'ŏnga ch'ulp'ansa, 1986.

Hoyt, James. *Soaring Phoenixes and Prancing Dragons.* Somerset, N.J.: Jimoondang, 2000.

Kim Chinyŏng and Ch'a Ch'unghwan. *Paeg'un kosa Yi Kyubo shijip.* Seoul: Minsok wŏn, 1997.

Kim Chonggil and Lee Ŏryŏng, editors. *Uriŭi myŏngshi.* Seoul: Tonga ch'ulp'ansa, 1990.

Kim Yong, compiler. *Uri kojŏn shiga hanmadang.* Seoul: Hyemun sŏgwan, 1994.

Lee Chongmuk. *Han'guk hanshiŭi chŏnt'onggwa munyemi.* Seoul: T'aehak sa, 2003.

Liu, James. *The Art of Chinese Poetry.* Chicago and London: University of Chicago Press, 1966.

O'Rourke, Kevin. *A Hundred Love Poems from Old Korea.* Folkestone: Global Oriental, 2005.

————. *Singing Like a Cricket, Hooting Like an Owl (Selected Poems of Yi Kyubo).* Ithaca: Cornell East Asia Program, 1995.

————, translator and editor. *Tilting the Jar, Spilling the Moon.* Seoul: UPA, 1988; Dublin: Dedalus Press, 1993.

Taedong shisŏn. Photoprint. Seoul: Hangmin ch'ulp'ansa, 1992.

Yang T'aesun. *Han'guk kojŏn shigaŭi chonghapchŏk koch'al.* Seoul: Minsok wŏn, 2003.

Yi Kyubo. *Tongguk Yi Sangguk chip.* Edited by Yi Ham, 1241. MS.

SHIJO

Ch'oe Tong'wŏn. *Koshijo non'go.* Seoul: Samyŏng sa, 1990.

Cho Kyuik. *Kagokch'angsaŭi kungmunhakchŏk ponjil.* Seoul: Chimmundang, 1994.

Chŏng Pyŏng'uk. *Shijo munhak sajŏn.* Seoul: Shin'gu munhwasa, 1974.

Hoyt, James. *Soaring Phoenixes and Prancing Dragons.* Somerset, N. J.: Jimoondang, 2000.

Kim Hŭnggyu. *Understanding Korean Literature.* Translated by Robert J. Fouser. New York: Sharpe, 1987.

Kungmun hakhoe, ed. *Koshijo yŏn'gu.* Seoul: Taehak sa, 1997.

Lee, Peter. *Korean Literature—Topics and Themes.* Tucson: University of Arizona Press, 1965.

O'Rourke, Kevin. *The Book of Korean Shijo*. Cambridge, Mass.: Harvard University Asia Center, 2002.

———. *A Hundred Love Poems from Old Korea*. Folkestone: Global Oriental, 2005.

———. *The Shijo Tradition*. Seoul: Jung Eum Sa, 1987.

Pak Ŭlsu. *Han'guk shijo taesajŏn*. Seoul: Asea munhwasa, 1992.

Rutt, Richard. *The Bamboo Grove*. Berkeley: University of California Press, 1971.

Shim Chaewan. *Shijoŭi munhŏnjŏk yŏn'gu*. Seoul: Sejong munhwasa, 1972.

———. *Yŏkdae shijo chŏnsŏ*. (Compendium of Shijo through the Ages). Seoul: Sejong munhwasa, 1972.

INDEX TO POETS

INDEX TO TITLES

INDEX TO FIRST LINES

How green the grass on the long bank
   now that the rain has cleared, 54
I am an old scholar, 69
I chanced on clear waters and looked
   therein, 77
I have a young daughter, 66
I knew nothing of the fierce wind and
   rain of the Fifth Watch, 75
I know you've come across the sea from
   home, 8
I long, I long, 35
I love Tao Yuanming, 65
I love the honorable bamboo, 78
I pass the temple on Ch'ŏnho san three
   times a year, 79
I put down the wine jar in front of Long
   Life Gate, 84
I put on my light summer coat and lie
   down, 62
I raise the glass bead curtain, embrace
   the mountain light, 78
I reveled all night, 21
I waken from dreams, 83
I wanted to bloom with spring blos-
   soms, 62
I was washing my silks by the willow
   stream, 82
Ignorant of my true self, 20
I'm forty-four now, 70
I'm over seventy now, 61
I'm sitting alone at the edge of the
   pond, 76
I'm the quiet type, 85
I'm worn out by tears, 18
In my youth I used to write songs, 59
In one hand I grasped a bramble, 80

In tears I long for my love, 24
In the glory days of Shilla, 30
In the old wandering, carefree days, 64
It rained and faired, then the snow flew
   thick, 43
It's never been possible to fabricate na-
   ture, 85
A Kangnam girl, flower pinned in her
   hair, 88
The king is father, 17
Kŏmun'go, books, and a grass-roof hut,
   83
Last night it rained on Pine Pavilion, 55
Last year when the chrysanthemums
   bloomed on Dragon Mountain, 83
Lodged in the hostelry; late autumn
   rain falling, 8
Long, long ago, a mirage was seen over
   a fortress, 12
Lord turtle, lord turtle, 4
Mid-spring—the hermitage is crystal
   clean—not a mote, 76
Mid-spring; the old hermitage was
   quiet, 76
Moon, 19, 25
The moon stands out against the gelid
   blue of sky after the rain has cleared,
   72
Moonlight filling the yard is a smoke-
   less candle, 78
Moonlight white on white pear blos-
   soms, 81
The mountain is rough rock layers and
   strange shaped stones, 53
A mountain monk coveted the moon,
   61